W9-BJJ-108

"Harley Gordon has been our 'go to' trusted source of timely and respected information for more than twenty-five years."

-Ken & Daria Dolan
"America's First Family of Personal Finance" and former television hosts on CNN, CNN.fn and CNBC

"...a very insightful book as to why families need to have a conversation with a loved one regarding long-term care..."

-Vincent Russo
Past President of The National Academy of Elder Law Attorneys

"This is a must read for anyone in middle age, who loves someone, and wants them protected from any event..."

-Dale Bell
Producer of the Academy Award-Winning film *Woodstock* and Emmy Award-winning PBS documentary, *And Thou Shalt Honor*

—— THE ——
CONVERSATION

HELPING SOMEONE YOU LOVE
PLAN FOR AN
EXTENDED CARE EVENT

— HARLEY GORDON —

FOREWORD BY ACADEMY AWARD WINNER
DALE BELL

DISCLAIMER

The content of this book is intended to be an introduction on long-term care (also known as extended care) topics that can play a role in your financial planning. It is not a substitute for personalized advice from a professional advisor. The information presented in this book is general and for educational purposes only and DOES NOT constitute financial, legal, investment, tax or accounting advice. The material presented may not be appropriate for your specific situation.

The book makes reference to various government programs and common provisions found in insurance policies. Congress may change the laws governing eligibility and benefit amounts for Medicare, Medicaid and other programs at any time. Every effort has been made to ensure this publication is as accurate as possible. However, no representations or warranties are made with respect to the accuracy or completeness of the contents of this book.

We strongly recommend that you seek the advice of a tax, legal, and financial services professional before making decisions related to any investment, insurance or other financial decisions. Neither the Publisher nor the Author is responsible for the consequences of any decisions or actions taken in reliance upon or as a result of the information provided in this book. Neither the author nor the Publisher can be held responsible for any direct or incidental loss resulting from applying any of the information provided or from any other source mentioned in the book.

Copyright © 2016 HARLEY GORDON

ISBN: 978-0-9972001-1-9

Back Cover, and Author Images © Harley Gordon - Dedication Image © Harley Gordon

All rights reserved. No part of this book may be reproduced or transmitted in any form or by any means, electronic or mechanical, including photocopying, recording, or by any information storage and retrieval system, without written permission of the author, except for the inclusion of brief quotations in a review.

Published by Acanthus Publishing, Boston, Massachusetts.

Reference herein to any commercial product, service, or company/organization by trade name, trademark, service mark, or other promotional language/imagery does not constitute or imply an endorsement or recommendation by HARLEY GORDON. The purpose of this promotional material, which appears on the back cover, is to encourage use of the book and concepts within certain companies/organizations. In all dealings with the insurance and financial services industries, HARLEY GORDON remains impartial and does not endorse a particular company, product, or service.

TABLE OF CONTENTS

- Thinking differently about the subject of extended care

- The necessity of creating a plan to protect those you love

- Misconceptions about long-term care insurance

- The proper use of an essential insurance product

- Different types of policies

- The proper way to engage someone you love in a conversation about extended care

- Sample conversations with a spouse, single parent, those in a second marriage, and same gender couples

• How to protect your finances in a crisis

Chapter 10: Auxiliary Legal Documents

• Why you need a power of attorney

• Why you need a health care proxy and living will

ACKNOWLEDGEMENTS

To my wife, Susan, and my children, Ian, Emily, Lily, and Benjamin for their love. The best things in life are not free, they are earned.

Special thanks to my mentors in the extended care world: Joe Pulitano, Joan Melanson, Jennifer White, Bill Comfort, John Fontana, and Skip Liddell.

To Ken and Daria Dolan, mentors and dear friends.

The author would like to acknowledge the insights provided by the Certified in Long-Term Care professional designation (further information available at *www.ltc-cltc.com*).

FOREWORD

"THE CONVERSATION" began for 400,000 people in 1969 on Max Yasgur's farm when Wavy Gravy stood on the stage in Woodstock, NY on Sunday morning to say: "We've got to feed and take care of each other!" Now years later, many of those Baby Boomers and their sisters and brothers who have spent their lives having fed and taken care of their children and those in need face a future they could little have imagined: having their children put aside potentially years of their lives to take care of them and the resulting consequences of doing so.

As I researched the state of caregiving in this country for the documentary *And Though Shalt Honor,* I realized just how difficult that burden is to children who have taken on the substantial responsibilities of adulthood. Although many step up to the challenge of providing what amounts to constant care for a frail parent, the consequences to themselves emotionally, physically, and financially and their families are, as Harley so aptly puts it, "...serious if not irreversible."

Since providing care to a parent or loved one often falls to a child it is essential that they be given the tools to talk to their parents about the impact of doing so. *The Conversation* provides these tools in a wholly unique way that gives parents the motivation to take action to protect their children. Harley's insight into how to talk to men in particular is groundbreaking.

This is a must read for anyone in middle age, who loves someone, and wants them protected from any event that could cause them harm.

–Dale Bell

Producer of Academy Award–winning documentary *Woodstock: The Movie* and Emmy Award–winning PBS documentary *And Though Shalt Honor*

INTRODUCTION

There are certain unexpected adversities in the life of a family that can leave an indelible mark. The death or serious disability of a child, spouse and/or parent with young children stands out, as does a child or children with special needs. In addition to these unexpected challenges, extended care must also be included. In fact, the argument can be made that there is a unique set of consequences from this event that separates it from the others.

The death or disability during working years of a spouse or parent almost always brings a family together to focus on surviving and overcoming the misfortune. The same can be said if a child has a severe disability. Yet the need for care, in so many cases, has the opposite effect. As you will see, it is very likely that it will tear families apart.

The death or disability of a spouse or parent during working years in many cases causes serious financial issues. However, in just as many cases, they find a way to put the pieces back together because they have the time, skills, and ability to work to do so. Paying for care has just the opposite effect: Chronic illnesses usually occur later in life, which means the ability to recover financially is severely restricted. This has both a short-term and long-term impact.

Short-term commitments, many of which families consider to be non-discretionary, cannot be kept because paying for care requires a reallocation of cash flow. Given the length of care, the eventuality is that there will be an intrusion into retirement funds, which has a direct effect on the ability to fulfill future commitments, such as to a surviving spouse, partner, children who depend on an inheritance, special needs children, or charities. In other words, not having a plan and properly funding it can disrupt all efforts to secure a sense of financial viability moving into the future.

There are solutions if a plan is in place. The problem is that very few avail themselves of the advice necessary to create that plan when they are healthy. That's because the subject is presented exclusively as a series of risks reinforced with statistics and pictures of frail and dependent individuals usually in nursing homes. Since by nature we have a deep-seated aversion to thinking about anything truly awful occurring, including a need for care, the result is that the subject is dismissed, that being more the case when an insurance product is trying to be sold to cover the event.

The Conversation is written for those who do not see the need for a plan. With few exceptions, the hesitators tend to be healthy men who have no prior experience in providing care. We hope to change your mind by fundamentally altering how the subject is framed. Gone is any mention of the risk of your needing care and the cost of paying for it. In its place will be a sobering look at the serious if not irreversible consequences providing care would have on those you love. The hope is that you will decide those consequences are too severe, thus prompting you to take action.

For those who are trying to have a conversation about the subject of long-term care (which is referred to as extended care) with someone you love, *The Conversation* will give you insight into why using risk as a motivating factor rarely works. It will be replaced with a series of talking points that can be integrated into a conversation that will ultimately compel that person to take action.

The Conversation is organized in a logical sequence to accomplish the above.

• **Chapter 1** explains extended care, the settings in which it is provided, and the consequences—emotional, physical, and financial—for those who must provide it.

• **Chapter 2** gives you insight into how to convey the consequences of providing care to those who do not believe the event will happen.

• **Chapters 3-6** speak to the necessity of creating a plan and then looking at the options for paying for it, including an in-depth analysis of self-funding, Medicare, the VA, and Medicaid.

• **Chapter 7** focuses on the use of long-term care insurance as an option to fund a plan. It includes an analysis of what these products actually do, which is contrary to what you may believe. In addition, readers are given insight into the tax benefits of owning long-term care insurance.

• **Chapter 8** takes the information you have learned and turns it into presentations for those you love. It includes talking to a parent, spouse, a couple in a second marriage, and partner.

• **Chapter 9** focuses on how to protect family resources in a crisis through the prudent use of Medicaid.

• **Chapter 10** examines two elements of auxiliary planning that are necessary to make sure the extended care plan that is created can be executed effectively, by eliminating uncertainty as to who has legal authority to carry out financial and medical directives. It includes a critical review of both powers of attorney and medical directives and who should and should not be appointed.

Finally, for those who look for guidance on how to talk about the subject, please be patient with those who find it difficult to hear what you are saying. It has nothing to do with being unreasonable or not caring for and loving you. In fact, it is just the opposite, as you will see.

Harley Gordon

DEDICATION

This book is personal. Lew Gordon's outlook on life was shaped by the Depression and tempered by service in World War II. After the war, he met Eleanor Shapiro at Winthrop Beach in Massachusetts and married her two years later. They set out to have children and thus become a family. I am the oldest of five.

Growing up, I never thought of my father as old. Truth is, I never thought of it at all even as I reached middle age. I had enough things to worry about, and the aging process treated both my father and mother benevolently. Until it didn't.

The call that changed my life and perspective on the subject of this book came in the mid-afternoon. My father had suffered a life-threatening stroke while undergoing a normal surgical procedure. Although he survived, it started a precipitous decline ending in dependency. What I learned as he needed increasing amounts of care is that he wasn't the problem; one way or the other he would be taken care of and kept safe.

The problem was that providing care was taking an emotional and physical toll on my mother. It got to the point that my brother Jon, seeing my mother buckle from the endless responsibility, put aside his life to help. The financial impact was serious as well, forcing my family to reallocate income and assets to help pay for care, raising the issue that my mother may not be able to remain financially stable at his death.

All of these consequences could have been mitigated if my father had put together a plan. However, like so many other healthy men, he thought it would never happen to him. In his mind, there was no risk of needing care and therefore no consequences to his family.

Conventional books and articles on the subject of extended care focus on the risk and cost of care, hoping it will motivate readers to take action, that action usually being the purchase of insurance. *The Conversation* takes a profoundly different approach. The book is not about what is going to happen to you. It makes no effort to scare you with statistics and frighten you into taking action.

Instead, this book is about your commitment to protect your family regardless of your age. It provides an inside look into the subject of extended care and provides the options you have to plan for it. It reveals the serious and often irreversible consequences providing care can have on those you invited into your life. Lastly, it gives you the tools to talk to your loved ones about extended care, even when they don't want to talk about it.

Extended care is the assistance needed when someone has a serious impairment. There are two types of impairments: physical and cognitive.

A physical impairment is the result of a chronic medical condition such as Parkinson's disease, multiple sclerosis, chronic pulmonary disease, and osteoporosis to name a few. Such impairments can be managed with medication and therapy but are never cured. As they progress, they have a direct impact on the activities of daily living (ADLs), the basic functions that we often take for granted. They include:

Bathing: Getting in or out of a bathtub or shower and washing.

Eating: Manipulating utensils and eating independently.

Dressing: Putting on clothes and being able to manipulate buttons and zippers.

Toileting: Using a toilet without assistance.

Continence: Bladder and bowel control.

Transferring: Moving from one place to another — from a bed to a chair or from the kitchen table to the couch, for example—without substantial assistance.

For someone whose mobility is diminished by a physical impairment illness or disability, these simple tasks become extremely difficult, or even impossible, without assistance.

A cognitive impairment is generally defined as a deterioration or loss of intellectual capacity, including:

- Short- or long-term memory

- Orientation as to person, place, and time

- Deductive or abstract reasoning

- Judgment as it relates to safety awareness

IMPAIRMENTS REQUIRE A SPECIAL LEVEL OF CARE

More than 90% of extended care is custodial in nature, generally defined as assistance with ADLs or supervision needed because the individual has a cognitive impairment. That is not to be confused with skilled care, defined as care so inherently complex it can only be administered under a plan of care created by a doctor and executed by nurses or their equivalent. By definition, skilled care plays a minor role in extended care settings.

CARE IS DELIVERED IN DIFFERENT SETTINGS

Providing care can be viewed as a continuum. In most cases, the effects of impairments start slowly and gradually escalate. Different accommodations and settings will be required as the illness progresses. Initially, care may be incidental and easily addressed at home by a spouse or family member. But as the condition worsens, the level and type of care become far more complex.

THE SETTINGS

HOME CARE

Given a choice, most Americans will elect to age in place. That is, they will use whatever services necessary to remain in their homes. Historically, aging in place was a practical alternative to nursing-home care, as long as the care needed was not intensive and an informal caregiver (usually a family member) was available. But times have changed.

Many factors enter into why the structure of caring for a family member who needs care and wants to remain at home becomes problematic. For instance, with the rise of dual-income households, it becomes increasingly difficult to provide what can amount to constant care. Then there's the issue of geography. Families are increasingly mobile, and although they can remain connected with technology, physical separation from other family members has a negative impact on the impaired individual's ability to remain at home.

Longevity is an increasingly important factor. Advances in medicine and medical care make it more likely that people will live longer with these illnesses, putting extraordinary stress on those who have no choice but to put their lives aside to make sure those they love are safe at home.

ADULT DAY CARE CENTERS

People who suffer from light to moderate impairments may benefit from adult day care centers, a form of non-skilled care that is often provided in a community setting. Adult day care centers, ironically, have little to do with the person who needs care, serving rather as respite for the caregiver. For example, an adult day care center allows the caregiver of an Alzheimer's patient a few hours off or provides a way for that caregiver to go to work.

ASSISTED-LIVING FACILITIES

Assisted-living facilities supply varying levels of assistance for people who have some trouble with daily activities but can, for the most part, still get through their daily routines or who have a mild cognitive impairment. The care is provided in a secure, home-like environment where residents live in individual apartments. Meals and services are provided in central social rooms. The level of care increases as the particular impairment takes its toll.

Individual units, or apartments, within assisted-living facilities are rented to the occupant. Costs vary, depending on geographic region. For information about costs in your area, contact the Commission on Accreditation of Rehabilitation Facilities or the Assisted Living Federation of America.

CONTINUING CARE RETIREMENT COMMUNITIES

A continuing care retirement community (CCRC), also known as a life-care community, is usually divided into three living components housed on one campus:

1. Independent living

2. Assisted living

3. Skilled nursing home

This built-in continuum of care allows residents to age in a familiar setting with the comfort of knowing they have access to increasing levels of care as their needs develop.

While assisted-living residents pay rent to live independently, CCRC residents enter into a contract with the facility that outlines how they will pay for and receive care for the duration of their lives. CCRC residents pay an entrance or buy-in fee, typically ranging from $200,000 to $400,000, as well as monthly fees.

The fee does not entitle the individual to own the unit, nor does he or she receive shares as in a cooperative. Rather, it is a license to live there. CCRCs have different policies regarding return of the entrance fee upon the resident's death or if he or she moves. The standard in the industry is to return 90% of the original amount. Because of the costs and contracts involved, it is best to consult with an attorney or financial professional before considering this type of facility.

INSTITUTIONAL CARE

HOSPITALS

Hospitals provide medical, not custodial, care. In the field of extended care, they generally act as gateways to long-term care services that usually begin with a short-term placement in a skilled nursing home. For example, if a patient is admitted to the hospital with a broken hip, he will be discharged after doctors determine that the fracture has been stabilized. If hospitalized for at least 72 hours, not including day of discharge, the patient qualifies for skilled or rehabilitative services in a nursing home for up to 100 days. Chapter 4 helps you understand how Medicare pays for these services.

NURSING HOMES

Nursing homes (also called *skilled nursing facilities*) provide three services:

1. Skilled care required by a prior stay in a hospital for a medical event

2. Rehabilitative services, which have the goal of helping the patient return to the community

3. Permanent placement because the patient cannot live safely at home or in the community

Nursing homes are licensed by both state and federal governments and must have qualified professionals on staff to attend to the needs of the patients.

A note about skilled nursing facilities:

If you were asked what you thought an extended care event was, no doubt the answer would be "old people in nursing homes." Likely, it's because when media outlets run stories on the subject, they invariably show images of... old people in nursing homes. Like winter follows fall, what comes next is the risk and cost of ending up in one.

Now if you are not old (or do not perceive yourself as being old) and consider yourself in fine health (even though your spouse or partner may suggest otherwise), why would these stories that focus on the risk motivate you to do anything other than to change the channel or turn the page?

The statistic often cited is that 43% of the population over 65 will need nursing home care. The survey, conducted by the *New England Journal of Medicine*, actually said that 43% of the population might spend some time in a facility, not the rest of their lives. The reality, however, is far different: Between the ages of 65 and 85, a weighted average of approximately only 3% of people will end their lives in one. Past the age of 85, the percentage increases to just 14%.

So why read further if (A) the risk is not high and (B) it's not going to happen to you in any event? Because extended care is not a series of illnesses that you experience that eventually cause you to end up in a nursing home.

Extended care is a life-changing event that imposes serious if not irreversible damages on those you invited into your life and promised to take care of.

THE CONSEQUENCES OF PROVIDING CARE

As the illness or illnesses progress, they so compromise you that in practical terms you are rendered unsafe. The result is an irony: Those who you said you would take care of have no choice but to place their lives aside to take care of you. Here are the predictable results:

EMOTIONAL AND PHYSICAL

By definition, extended care is all-consuming. Here are the cascading consequences:

• Providing care to you will make those you love as chronically ill as you are.

• If you have a child or children, at least one will put aside his or her life for two reasons: First, your spouse or partner will start to buckle from the constant stress of providing care. Second, you may be the surviving parent. While you surely do not want your child involved, the reality is, what choice will he or she have?

• If there is more than one child, it is very unlikely all of them will share the responsibility of helping you equally. This causes hard feelings between those who do and those who don't.

The result? There is a very real likelihood that the children may never speak to each other again.

FINANCIAL

Paying for care disrupts carefully thought plans to secure financial viability in the future.

Paying for care causes a reallocation of resources, starting with your income. The considerable problem is that it is likely that you are living on—or will need to live on in the future—a level of income that equals, or nearly equals, what you earned during your working years. Shifting your income to pay for care has a direct impact on your ability to keep financial commitments, which may include:

- Helping a child who has not made the best decisions in life

- Providing for a child with special needs

- Continuing obligations to a former spouse

- Helping pay for a grandchild's education

- Lifestyle expenses, including a vacation home, boat, and club memberships

- Continuing commitments to charities

- and more...

Although in theory many of these expenses may be considered discretionary, in the world of the successful, they are often the opposite: nondiscretionary. Asking income to both pay for care and cover nondiscretionary expenses is, for practical purposes, double counting it.

If the illness or illnesses last long enough, it invariably leads to an intrusion into your retirement portfolio, the sole purpose of which is to provide income. Using principal to pay for care subjects it to:

- **Untimely and unnecessary taxes:** The former occurs when cashing in an IRA or other pre-tax investment before it was planned. The latter means having your heirs pay a capital gains tax on appreciated assets you transfer to them to help pay for your care. If such assets were held in your name at death, none would be due because of a free step-up in basis.

• **Market timing:** Liquidating assets to pay for care when the market is down actualizes a paper loss.

• **Liquidity issues:** Is most of your net worth in illiquid investments such as a small business, real estate investment trusts, or a hedge fund? If so, it would be very difficult to use it to pay for care.

And just as important, every dollar used to pay for care is one dollar less to generate income to fulfill the above commitments.

Have you noticed that there has not been one mention of the risk of needing care or what it costs? That's because, like all healthy people, you have to believe that the most awful things in life, if they have to happen, will do so to others. Now, here's where gender comes into play. As you will see in the next chapter, men and women tend to respond differently to the risk of needing care. Therefore, a unique communication style is necessary for each gender.

POWER THOUGHTS

• The need for care is caused by impairments. As they progress, they so severely compromise you that you are no longer safe. That means those you promised to take care of have no choice but to put their lives aside to take care of you.

• There are two sets of consequences to those you love due to stress: emotional and physical. The stress is caused from providing care and financial support that demands a reallocation of income and assets.

• Providing care to you because of a chronic illness will make those who do so as chronically ill as you are.

• It is likely a child will have to put aside his or her life at great cost emotionally and physically. It will also impact the relationship with his or her family and siblings who may not help.

• Providing care does not bring families together. It tears them apart, causing irreversible consequences.

Not one of my clients who now needs care ever thought that it would happen to them. What they didn't understand is that extended care was not a series of risks that would happen to *them*, but rather a set of serious if not irreversible consequences that would happen to *those they love*.

Regardless of how serious the consequences of needing care are—and Chapter 1 set forth some serious issues—there is the possibility of taking steps to mitigate them with a plan, even if you don't think the event will occur. Chapter 2 is written from two perspectives: from that of a healthy male who believes he is the primary earner and protector, and from his spouse or partner who sees herself or himself as the primary provider of care.

How you respond to the risk of an unexpected serious event in life, such as dying, becoming disabled, or in this case needing extended care, is to a large degree determined by genetics. Any discussion that hopes to motivate someone you love to take action to mitigate the consequences of an extended care event depends on an understanding of what motivates the individual.

How a person responds to the issue of risk, i.e., whether they will create a plan to mitigate it, depends to a great degree on human evolution. Evolutionary psychology is the study of how the brain developed to allow our species to adapt to and ultimately survive in a hostile environment.[1]

Men's brains generally developed characteristics that favor:[2]

- **Coordination of movement**

- **Problem solving**

- **Spatial memory** (the ability to map and remember terrain)

- **Aggression**

- **Short-term focus**

- **A deep sense of invulnerability expressed in a disregard or minimizing of risk**[3]

These primal traits were essential for three reasons: personal survival, the ability to hunt, and protection for those they hunted for, their families.[4]

Women's brains generally developed different traits that favor:

- **Gathering and interpreting of auditory and visual information.** For example, they read different things into how a child is crying, leading them to take different actions.

- **Reading emotions**

- **Intuition**

- **A strong emotional quotient that makes it easier to bond to others**

- **An aversion to risk**

Taken as a whole, these traits serve as the foundation for raising, nurturing, and protecting children.

How men and women perceive risk dictates whether they will take steps to plan for it.

As stated above, men are generally hardwired to believe that they have two tasks to perform: find food to bring home and protect those in their home. Their brains are constructed to dismiss the risk of performing these tasks. It's natural, therefore, to dismiss the risk of needing extended care (or of dying, or becoming seriously disabled during working years for that matter) because it would undermine their basic directives. In fact, if you are a male and you believe your role is to provide for and protect others, do you think there is any chance of these events happening to you? From your perspective, the answer is likely "no."

Why? Because, like myself, you cannot imagine being unavailable to take care of those you love. Therefore, in your mind, the risk of an extended care event happening is essentially zero. In fact, any discussion of the subject likely makes you feel very uncomfortable. If there is little or no chance of these events happening, why take the time to create a plan to deal with it?

In other words, men tend to bifurcate the issue of risk and the subject of consequences; if there is no risk in the event happening, there can be, by rational deduction, no consequences.

Women view the issue of risk very differently. Although they also believe, as do men, that they will not need care (or die or become seriously disabled during working years), they are predisposed to take a more *nuanced approach* to the subject. As stated, they are usually the ones directly involved in the raising and nurturing of children. They instinctively understand the emotional, physical, and financial responsibilities. The result is that they view an unexpected need for care through an internal prism: They take the event and *refract* it into a kaleidoscope of *consequences*:

- They understand what the emotional and physical impact on their spouses and children would be if *they* needed care.

- They understand what the emotional, physical, and financial consequences would be to themselves and their children if their *spouses* needed care.

Unlike men, who see risk and the consequences of a risk as being separate, women generally see them as a singularity: A risk is a consequence. Think about it this way, gentleman: Have you ever tossed your young child into the air? Awesome, no? Your wife's reaction: A series of vignettes of what happens if you don't catch your child.

Men generally believe there are no *ifs*, *ands*, or *buts* of needing care. Women, when asked if they believe they will need care, will often hesitate and then answer... *they hope they don't need care.*

While genetics plays a major role in one's perspective on needing care, how a person perceives his or her role in the family matters as well. For example, there are many women who are primary financial providers or in professions such as law enforcement or the military. Their husbands or partners may be the primary providers of care. Perhaps women in these roles view risk as men would, and men vice versa. It is no different with same-sex couples. The question is how the individual is genetically predisposed to the issue of risk.

A LOOK AT TRADITIONAL CONVERSATIONS

Since the majority of procrastination regarding planning for unexpected serious events in life is practiced by men (and some women), the focus at this point is helping those people trying to get them to take it seriously: their wives, children, and/or partners.

If you are a woman and have tried to motivate your husband, partner, or father to create an extended care plan, you have generally employed two tactics: Citing studies supplied by the popular press to make the point that care is likely necessary based on statistics and its expense. Or, reminding him of your prior experience taking care of your parents or his, and the resulting stress. It's doubtful either of these approaches have worked, which is why you invested in this book.

Men believe that their responsibility is to provide for and protect those they love. As such, they are blind to the alternative. In fact, any suggestion by you that he may not be able to provide for his family due to a need for care, regardless of how factually correct, will make him quite uncomfortable. This causes something called cognitive dissonance, which is the discomfort experienced when one's beliefs or values are challenged or undermined by facts or conduct to the contrary. There are three ways someone can resolve the discomfort:

1. Ignore that which makes you uncomfortable: Simply stop reading or thinking about anything that makes you uncomfortable.

2. Rationalize behavior: Come up with ideas that allow you to continue to think as you do.

3. Change behavior: Change your beliefs so they do not conflict with the facts or conduct that caused the discomfort.

A classic example of cognitive dissonance is smoking. Those who smoke believe it gives them pleasure. The issue, of course, is that there is ample evidence that smoking will cause any number of illnesses likely shortening one's lifespan. When confronted with these inconvenient facts, smokers respond in one of the following manners:

1. Ignore the facts: Simply stop reading the

studies or cut people off when they start making a speech about it.

2. Rationalize behavior: "If I stop smoking, I'll put weight on"; "Everyone has to die of something"; "I know someone whose father-in-law smoked three packs of Camels a day and outlived all of his friends who exercised."

3. Change behavior: Simply stop smoking, which of course is not so simple.

Any discussion of the risk of needing care will almost certainly cause men to become uncomfortable, because it undermines their belief that nothing is going to happen. There are three ways they can and have likely reacted when you have tried to discuss the subject:

1. Ignore the facts: Listen politely and then do... nothing.

2. Rationalize behavior: "I am too young to think about it"; "I know it's important but I have other more important things to think about"; "I am not going to need care"; "No one in my family has ever needed care"; "I'll put a gun in my mouth if it happens."

3. Change behavior: Simply change their belief.

If you have ever tried to discuss the subject of extended care, you likely have been the recipient of these statements or inaction. Any attempt to elicit a favorable response to a conversation about extended care must start with an understanding of what motivates decent men to create a family or help others. Only then can an appropriate set of guidelines be created to engage them in a conversation that will motivate them to take positive action.

A number of studies conducted on what motivates men to create families show conclusively that they want to take care of someone and make a difference in their lives.[5] This reinforces their belief that they are providers and protectors of others. While they will not respond to protecting themselves from any risk—let alone the risk of needing care—they will, if approached correctly, respond to any threat that undermines their ability to take care of their family. In this case, that threat is a series of serious if not irreversible consequences for those they love if care was ever needed.

The conversation, therefore, has to focus not on a series of risks to him, regardless of whether they are factually true, but only on a series of consequences to them.

If you are a woman trying to have a conversation on the subject, it starts with a statement that at first appears to be counterproductive—mentioning to your husband, partner, or father that this is not a discussion based on his needing care. It may seem counterproductive to you, because you see the risk and consequences of needing care as one in the same. Remember, however, that to him they are two separate issues. If you start the conversation with the risk of the event happening, you will create cognitive dissonance, causing him to shut down or come up with the types of objections previously stated.

However, by starting a conversation with the counter-intuitive statement that this is not about the risk of needing care, you have accomplished a milestone. Not only does he not shut down, he is compelled to ask you what you mean. Whenever you can begin the conversation with that statement, you can continue it. As you will see in Chapter 8, all conversations begin with this statement.

When asked "What do you mean," continue by explaining that this is not a discussion about a series of risks that he faces as he ages, but rather a discussion about a series of consequences to yourself, the children, and your ability to fulfill financial commitments *if* care is needed. Chapter 8 integrates those consequences outlined in Chapter 1 into powerful thoughts that compel him to take action to protect you and the children or others.

So what have you just accomplished? Something special. You have engaged someone who didn't want to talk to you about the subject of needing care in the first place and brought him to a place where he is willing to take affirmative steps. You have done so by reconciling two seemingly irreconcilable beliefs in a man's brain.

There is one side of his brain that is figuratively atavistic in nature. It is driven by a will to survive, which is enhanced by not thinking about risk. There is a voice on that side that tells him not to listen to your discussion of what's going to happen as he ages. There is, however, another side, one that is prone to take action despite the absence of risk. That side is motivated by his conscience, where the voice keeps nagging him with the uncomfortable question "what if"—"What would happen to those you promised to take care of if you did need care?"

If the conversation is conducted properly, it still allows him to believe nothing will happen, that the risk remains at zero percent. However, he stops measuring the risk of the event and instead focuses on the consequences to those he loves and concludes they are one hundred percent to them, i.e., unacceptable. That will be expressed in statements such as "I never thought about it like that," "Are you serious," and "I don't want that to happen."

The next step is to suggest that the best way to protect his family is to put together a plan. The purpose of a plan is not to protect the person you are talking to (remember he still believes he won't need care) but those he cares enough about.

THE PLAN

The plan is to allow you to remain safe at home for as long as possible while protecting the emotional, physical, and financial wellbeing of those you love.

This is accomplished by mitigating the two sets of consequences endemic to providing care. You want to be able to hire professionals to provide the care, thereby minimizing the emotional and physical stress on your spouse, partner, or child. Second, you want to mitigate the cost of paying for that care. This can be effectively done with a form of long-term care insurance. Chapters 3 through 6 look at other forms of paying for the plan.

POWER THOUGHTS

• How people respond to the issue of risk, i.e., whether they will create a plan to mitigate it, depends to a great degree on human evolution. Evolutionary psychology is the study of how the brain developed to allow our species to adapt to and ultimately survive in a hostile environment.

• Men are wired to minimize if not dismiss risk in life. If there is no risk of a serious event happening, what consequences can there be? If there are no consequences, why put together a plan?

• Women have an aversion to risk. They see the risk of a serious event and the consequences of it as being inseparable. The result...

• Men generally believe there are no *ifs, ands,* or *buts* of needing care. Women, when asked if they believe they will need care, will often hesitate and then answer... **they hope they don't need care.**

• Using risk to motivate men to create a plan never works because they deeply believe care will never be needed. In fact, it causes cognitive dissonance leading to a shutdown of the conversation.

• Changing the focus of the conversation from a series of risks he faces to a series of consequences to those he loves compels him to consider what would happen to them if he failed to take action.

REFERENCES

1.) Leda Cosmides and John Tooby, "Evolutionary Psychology: A Primer," *Center for Evolutionary Psychology*, January 13, 1997, http://www.cep.ucsb.edu/primer.html.

2.) Simon Baron-Cohen, *The Essential Difference: Male And Female Brains And The Truth About Autism* (New York: Basic Books, 2003).

Madhura Ingalhalikar, Alex Smith, Drew Parker, Theodore D. Satterthwaite, Mark A. Elliott, Kosha Ruparel, Hakon Hakonarson, Raquel E. Gur, Ruben C. Gur, and Ragini Verma, "Sex Differences in the Structural Connectome of the Human Brain," *Proceedings of the National Academy of Sciences of the United States* 111, no. 2 (2013): 823.

3.) Doreen Kimura, "Sex Differences in the Brain," *Scientific American* 12, no. 1s (2002): 32.

Deborah Blum, *Sex on the Brain: The Biological Differences between Men and Women* (New York: Penguin Books, 1997).

Christine Harris and Michael Jenkins, "Gender Differences in Risk Assessment: Why Do Women Take Fewer Risks than Men?" *Judgment and Decision Making* 1, no. 1 (2006): 48.

4.) Michael Gurven and Kim Hill, "Why Do Men Hunt?" *Current Anthropology* 50, no. 1 (2009): 51.

5.) James Stenson, *Father, the Family Protector* (New York: Scepter Publishers, 2010).

Now that the plan is established, the next step is to consider what will fund it. Chapter 3 reviews the most common beliefs about self-funding that consumers have about paying for care.

SELF-FUNDING

SELF-FUNDING YOUR PLAN TO PROTECT YOUR FAMILY

The longest period of care is generally for those with dementia. The average life expectancy, after diagnosis, is generally between 6 and 10 years. That includes the beginning stages, in which the individual becomes forgetful but can still navigate the daily routines of life and remain safe at home with little assistance.

A reasonable period of dependency would be about 5–6 years. The traditional approach taken by advisors and the popular media is that an individual with investible assets of about $1.5 million would be able to cover the cost. No doubt. A couple of thoughts, however, that you may want to consider are as follows.

ASSETS DO NOT PAY FOR CARE, INCOME DOES

Consider paying for care as just another expense in life. Expenses should be paid for not from capital but from cash flow. The problem is that you are likely living on most if not all of your income in later years to cover what amounts to nondiscretionary expenses. For example, which of the following are discretionary expenses—i.e., can easily be discontinued if care is needed?

- Providing financial assistance to a child who needs it

- Funding a 529 college fund for a grandchild or grandchildren

- Family vacations

- Contributions to a charity in the form of gifts or tithing

- A vacation home or boat

- Providing for a child with special needs, if applicable

My experience tells me that these are not discretionary. That is, you would want to keep these commitments even if you needed care. However, expecting cash flow to both pay for care and cover the nondiscretionary expenses is, in effect, double counting it.

Many clients have sufficient assets, which I refer to as capital, to pay for care. But then I remind them of the purpose of capital: to generate income.

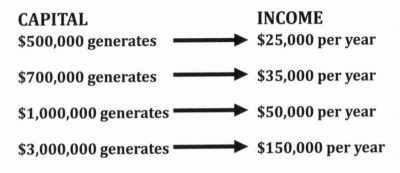

CAPITAL		INCOME
$500,000 generates	→	$25,000 per year
$700,000 generates	→	$35,000 per year
$1,000,000 generates	→	$50,000 per year
$3,000,000 generates	→	$150,000 per year

(Based on a 5% interest rate)

If you are in your late 50s or older, it's likely that the right side of the equation is of interest to you; you are not focused as much on the amount of assets or capital but rather on what it will generate in the future as income. Using capital to pay for care disrupts the purpose of the portfolio: to generate predictable streams of income. It also creates the following issues:

• **Liquidity:** Can cash be raised to pay for care, and if so, would assets have to be sold at a loss?

• **Market conditions:** Paying for care may end up actualizing a loss.

- **Taxes:** Liquidating qualified assets or low-cost-based assets creates unnecessary taxes.

- **Legacy assets:** Would family property have to be sold or could it continue to be supported?

- **Philanthropy:** Inability or reduced ability to leave a charitable bequest.

And every **capital** dollar used to pay for care is one less dollar available to generate income.

"If I need care, I won't have much of a lifestyle anyway. The money I save can be used to pay for care."

Not necessarily. Let's play that thought out, starting with your lifestyle. If you have achieved financial success, it likely includes financial commitments such as those to charities, social clubs, contributions to 529 accounts, helping your child, and vacations to name just a few. In other words, your lifestyle is inextricably woven into that of your family.

A SPECIAL CASE: PAYING FOR CARE AND COMMITMENTS TO CHARITIES

Charitable endeavors are perhaps the most powerful case you can make against self-funding. A 2009 Harvard Business School study, *Feeling Good about Giving*, listed three reasons why people make a financial commitment to a charity:

- Sustaining a purpose in life

- Combating social injustice

- Selfless giving is a key component to many spiritual and religious belief systems

It is not unreasonable to assume that these commitments are not discretionary. What are the consequences of choosing to self-fund the cost of care for charitable giving?

- Every $1.00 used to pay for care is $1.00 less a charity receives.

- Every $1.00 used to pay for care deprives the individual of a charitable deduction.

In other words, using income *and capital* to pay for care disrupts every plan you have created to secure a sense of financial viability moving into future years.

POWER THOUGHTS

• Assets do not pay for care, income does. Reallocating it directly impacts your ability to keep financial commitments.

• Using assets, which is really capital in nature, disrupts every plan to secure a sense of financial viability moving into the future.

• Just because you need care doesn't mean your financial commitments end.

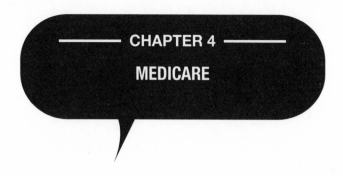

WILL MEDICARE FUND YOUR PLAN?[1]

The simple answer is no. Medicare is health insurance. Extended care requires custodial care, as explained in Chapter 1. That said, this chapter is a useful review of what Medicare will and will not cover.

MEDICARE BENEFITS

Medicare[2] is an entitlement program that provides a health insurance plan for people age 65 and older, disabled people, and people of any age with end-stage renal disease (ESRD; permanent kidney failure requiring dialysis or a kidney transplant). It is administered by the Centers for Medicare and Medicaid Services (CMS) and consists of four parts:

1. Parts A and B, also called Original Medicare

2. Part C, also called Medicare Advantage

3. Part D, also called the Prescription Drug Program

Medicare Parts A, B, and C cover skilled and rehabilitative care. Part D covers prescription medication.

SKILLED CARE

Skilled care is defined as "services provided by, or under the supervision of, licensed nursing personnel." It can be performed in a hospital, subacute or skilled nursing facility, or at home. All care must be administered under an individual plan of care.

To meet Medicare's skilled care definition, a person must require at least one of the following: IVs, muscular injections on a regular basis, tube feeding, physical therapy, speech therapy, continuous oxygen, treatment of deep skin lesions, suctioning, or close monitoring on a round-the-clock basis.

REHABILITATIVE CARE

Rehabilitative care is a form of skilled care; there is no need for rehabilitative services unless there is an underlying medical event requiring skilled services. The goal of rehabilitative services is to put the patient back, as much as possible, in the position he or she was in prior to the medical event. The services are administered under a plan, which includes ascertainable goals.

CUSTODIAL CARE

Many consumers believe that Medicare will pay for extended care. In many ways, it did even though there was never a mandate to do so. It is therefore necessary to explain the program and what steps Medicare has taken to end what it considered to be abusive tactics.

MEDICARE PART A: HOSPITAL INSURANCE PROGRAM

A *covered worker*—a person who has worked and paid Social Security taxes—becomes eligible for Part A at age 65. The covered worker may have to pay a premium if, over his or her lifetime, the worker or the worker's spouse has not accumulated sufficient employment on which Social Security taxes were paid. Employment is measured in *credits:* one credit is given for each $1,000 earned, up to a maximum of four credits per calendar year.[3]

Although workers may retire at age 62 and qualify for Social Security retirement benefits (albeit reduced), they qualify for Medicare Part A only at age 65. Covered workers also become eligible for Medicare if they have qualified for Social Security Disability Income (SSDI) benefits for at least two years or if they permanently require kidney dialysis.

Part A imposes deductibles and coinsurance payments, which are discussed later in this chapter. Medicare Part B, also reviewed later, is a voluntary program that requires a monthly premium.

Part A benefits include:

- Inpatient hospital care deductibles and co-insurance in 2016

- A deductible of $1,288

- A copayment of $322 per day for days 61–90

- A copayment of $644 per lifetime reserve day (of 60 days)

- Skilled nursing-home care

- Medically necessary home health care

- Hospice care

- Blood transfusion

INPATIENT HOSPITALIZATION

Medicare Part A covers reasonable charges for semi-private rooms in accredited hospitals. Part A covers only charges billed by the hospital; it does not cover charges of physicians, surgeons, or anesthesiologists providing services in the hospital. Those services are covered through Medicare Part B.

Benefit limits are applied to each *benefit period*. A new benefit period begins after the patient has been out of the hospital for at least 60 days.

Aside from the deductible amounts, which are the patient's responsibility, full hospital charges are covered for the first 60 days of a benefit period. Coverage scales down from the 61st to the 90th day and ceases thereafter. However, recipients have an additional 60-day lifetime reserve that they can use if necessary.

Prior to 1983, Medicare's rules approved paying hospitals any "reasonable costs" for Medicare patients entering a hospital. Essentially, any Medicare patient needing hospital care was allowed to stay in a hospital until he or she fully recuperated.

Faced with burgeoning costs in the 1980s that threatened future benefits, Medicare changed its rules on reimbursement to hospitals and adopted a price-tag system of reimbursement—the Prospective Payment System (PPS). Under PPS, hospitals are paid a predetermined rate for inpatient hospital care furnished to Medicare Part A beneficiaries. Hospitals are thus under pressure to keep their actual costs of treating Medicare patients under the program's fixed reimbursement level.[4]

SKILLED NURSING FACILITY CARE

Medicare Part A covers care provided through skilled nursing facilities (SNFs). The full cost of such care is covered for the first 20 days. A daily deductible of $161 in 2016 is applied for care received from the 21st to the 100th day. Coverage ceases after 100 days.

These rules imply that Medicare would pay for extended care, at least in part, for up to 100 days. That is not always true. Four conditions must be met to qualify for what Medicare calls *extended care coverage*:

1. The beneficiary must first have received inpatient hospital care for at least three nights and entered a skilled nursing-home facility within 30 days of that hospital stay.[5]

2. He or she must be entering the facility for the same medical reason that required the hospital stay.

3. The care must be *skilled*, defined as "services so inherently complex that they can be safely and effectively performed only by, or under

the supervision of, technical or professional personnel."

4. The patient must be receiving rehabilitative care under a plan with ascertainable goals.

The full entitlement to 100 skilled nursing facility benefit days is renewed each time the individual begins a new benefit period. A new benefit period begins when the beneficiary has gone 60 days without hospital or SNF care.

Prior to July 1, 1998, the above care was paid for on a fee-for-service basis. The SNF simply billed Medicare (through a fiscal intermediary) for the services, and Medicare in turn paid the bill. The average Medicare-funded stay in a skilled nursing facility was approximately 50 days.

Medicare switched SNFs to a flat-fee payment system in 1998. Reimbursement is now based on the Prospective Payment System used for hospitals. Like a hospital, if an SNF can provide the care for less than the amount paid by Medicare, it keeps the difference. If not, it absorbs the loss.

MEDICARE PART B: MEDICAL INSURANCE

Medicare Part B is a voluntary program that Medicare beneficiaries must elect when they become eligible for Part A. Beneficiaries who decline Part B coverage when they first become eligible may enroll later but at a higher premium, unless the reason for the delay was continued employment. The premiums for Part B coverage, which are based on income, are deducted from the beneficiary's monthly Social Security retirement income check. In 2016, the Part B premium (without the penalty for delayed enrollment) are shown in Table 1.

Table 1. Medicare Part B monthly premium 2016		
Single	**Joint Filing**	**Premium**
$85,000 or less	$170,000 or less	$121.80
$85,001–$107,000	$170,000–$214,000	$170.50
$107,001–$160,000	$214,001–$320,000	$243.60
$160,001–$214,000	$320,001–$428,000	$316.70
Above $214,000	Above $428,000	$389.80

Part B benefits (subject to deductible and coinsurance limits) include:

- **Physician services**

- **Outpatient hospital care**

- **Home care services not covered in Part A**

- **Surgical services and supplies**

- **Physical and speech therapy**

- **Ambulance trips**

- **Diagnostic tests**

- **Durable medical equipment**

- **Prosthetic devices**

- **Blood transfusion**

Table 2. Medicare Part B deductibles and coinsurance in 2016	
Service	**Patient's responsibility**
Physicians' services	$166 + 20% of the Medicare-approved amount
Outpatient mental services	45% of the Medicare-approved amount after $166 deductible
Durable medical equipment	20% of the Medicare-approved amount
Blood	First 3 pints + $166 deductible + 20% of any additional Medicare-approved amount

The deductible and coinsurance requirements are shown in Table 2.

The deductible applies only once per year for any Part B service received.

MEDICARE PAYMENT OF HOME HEALTH CARE COSTS

As with Part A, Part B will cover home health services, which include limited reasonable and only medically necessary part-time care and services such as skilled nursing care, physical or occupational therapy, home health aide services, speech-language pathology, and medical social services. It also includes certain home-use medical equipment (wheelchairs, hospital beds, walkers, oxygen) and other medical supplies.

Home health services are reimbursed on four conditions:

1. Your physician must decide that you need medical care at home and make a plan for your care at home.

2. You must need intermittent skilled nursing care, physical therapy, speech-language therapy, or to continue occupational therapy.

3. The home health agency must be Medicare certified.

4. You must be homebound, or normally unable to leave home without help. To be homebound means that leaving home takes considerable and taxing effort. You can be homebound and still leave home for medical treatment or short, infrequent absences for non-medical reasons, such as trips to a barber or church. A need for adult day care does not keep you from getting

home health care.

Medicare covers the following services to beneficiaries meeting these conditions:

- Part-time or intermittent nursing care provided by, or under the supervision of, a registered professional nurse

- Physical, occupational, or speech therapy

- Medical social services under the direction of a physician

- Part-time or intermittent services of a personal-care attendant, related to skilled care provided by a nurse

Medicare does not cover the following:

- 24-hour-a-day care at home

- Meals delivered to the home

- Homemaker services

- Personal-care attendants who assist the patient with daily activities

THE CONVERSATION • HARLEY GORDON

In other words, Medicare does not cover custodial care.

Medicare also covers durable medical equipment acquired for at-home use, except for a 20% copayment. Medicare requires the use of Medicare-certified home health care agencies and poses other requirements.

MEDICARE EXTENDS REFORM TO HOME HEALTH CARE

Prior to January 1, 1998, both Parts A and B covered what amounted to an unlimited number of home health care visits, without coinsurance or deductible requirements, when beneficiaries met the above conditions.[6] Providing services for extended periods of time was possible because providers were paid on a fee-for-service basis.

This ended on January 1, 1998, when, in accordance with the Balanced Budget Act of 1997, Medicare started reimbursing home health care agencies on a flat-fee basis, as it already did for skilled nursing home care. The impact was immediate.[7] Providers are now prospectively paid a flat fee for care based on a set of diagnostic criteria. There is no incentive to provide any more care than is necessary.

In summation, Congress is bringing Medicare back to its roots: paying for skilled and rehabilitative care, not custodial care.

MEDICARE PART C: MEDICARE ADVANTAGE[8]

Medicare offers beneficiaries the option of receiving coverage through private health care plans. Known as Medicare Part C, or Medicare Advantage, this is an attempt by the government to move from a fee-for-service basis to a fixed-cost one by paying a provider a flat fee per enrolled beneficiary. The provider, in turn, makes money by promoting preventive care, negotiating discounts, and controlling expenses—like a traditional private-sector insurer. The insured is offered a variety of plans that best suit his or her health needs and cover more services (thus obviating the need for Medicare supplement insurance), at a cost that is generally less than fee-for-service under Parts A and B. Regardless of the plan, the insured must retain Part C coverage.

Three types of plans are available:

1. Health Maintenance Organizations (HMOs)

2. Preferred Provider Organizations (PPOs)

3. Private Fee-for-Service Plans (PFFS plans)

Although HMOs are required to provide the full range of benefits offered by fee-for-service Parts A and B, they do so through a prearranged network of providers. An HMO appeals to cost-conscious individuals who like the additional benefits, such as prescription eyeglasses and preventive services. Some HMOs charge a monthly fee in addition to the Medicare premiums.

MEDICARE SUPPLEMENT INSURANCE: MEDIGAP INSURANCE

Medigap insurance is privately sold insurance that, as its name suggests, covers gaps in Medicare coverage. Although privately offered, it is highly regulated by the federal government. For example, it is not designed to work with Medicare Advantage,[9] the Medicare Prescription Drug Program, nor with tax-free Medicare medical savings accounts (MSAs). Medigap is standardized into eight plans in all but three states, which use their own standardization.

Like the Medicare program[10] itself, however, Medigap policies do not pay for custodial care.

MEDICARE PRESCRIPTION DRUG PROGRAM[11]

Starting January 1, 2006, Medicare beneficiaries, regardless of income, health status, or prescription drug usage, gained access to prescription drug coverage. Medicare contracts with private companies, which offer a variety of coverage options; the more benefits, the higher the cost. Medicare prescription drug plans are voluntary.

Part D is guaranteed-issue, but if the beneficiary does not enroll within a prescribed period after reaching 65, the beneficiary is penalized 1% per month times the average monthly national premium until he or she does enroll and pays the higher amount thereafter.

In general, Part D works as follows: An enrollee pays a monthly premium in addition to any premium for Medicare Part A and Part B. Regardless of the plan, in

2016 the participant will usually pay:

1. The first $360 per year for prescriptions, although some plans may cover this.

2. After the $360 yearly deductible, the participant pays 25% of yearly drug costs from $360 to $3,310. The plan pays the remaining 75% of the costs.

3. Once you have spent $4,850 in bills (so-called doughnut hole) catastrophic coverage applies: The plan generally pays 95% of further bills.

POWER THOUGHTS

• Medicare is health insurance that pays for skilled and rehabilitative care. Extended care requires custodial care, which is assistance with activities of daily living or supervision because of a severe cognitive condition.

• Medicare will not pay for custodial care.

REFERENCES

1.) *The Corporation for Long-Term Care Certification*, Inc., 2016, https://www.ltc-cltc.com/.

2.) Centers for Medicare & Medicaid Services, *Medicare & You 2016* (Washington, DC: US Department of Health and Human Services, 2015), https://www.medicare.gov/Pubs/pdf/10050.pdf.

3.) 42 U.S.C. § 1395c.

42 U.S.C. § 1395d.

4.) 42 U.S.C. § 1395ww (d).

5.) "Coverage of Extended Care (SNF) Services under Hospital Insurance," *Medicare Benefit Policy Manual* (Baltimore, MD: Centers for Medicare & Medicaid Services, 2015), https://www.cms.gov/Regulations-and-Guidance/Guidance/Manuals/downloads/bp102c08.pdf.

6.) *Part A Medicare Intermediary Manual* (Pub. 13).

Part B Medicare Carrier Manual (Pub. 14)

7.) Rachel L. Murkofsky, Russell S. Phillips, Ellen P. McCarthy, Roger B. Davis, and Mary Beth Hamel, "Length of Stay in Home Care Before and After the 1997 Balanced Budget Act," *Journal of the American Medical Association* 289, no. 21 (2003): 2841.

8.) "Medicare Advantage," *The Henry J. Kaiser Family Foundation*, June 29, 2015, http://kff.org/medicare/fact-sheet/medicare-advantage/.

9.) Centers for Medicare & Medicaid Services, "Medigap & Medicare Advantage Plans," *Medicare.gov*, https://www.medicare.gov/supplement-other-insurance/medigap/medigap-and-medicare-advantage/medigap-and-medicare-advantage-plans.html.

10.) Centers for Medicare & Medicaid Services, "What's Medicare Supplement Insurance (Medigap)?" *Medicare.gov*, https://www.medicare.gov/supplement-other-insurance/medigap/whats-medigap.html.

11.) Centers for Medicare & Medicaid Services, *Medicare.gov*, https://www.medicare.gov/.

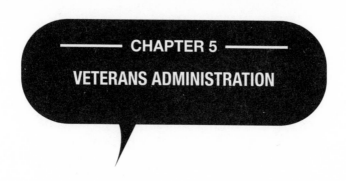

Will the Department of Veterans Affairs pay for my plan?

Generally the answer is no. The following is a comprehensive analysis of the benefits offered to veterans, retired military, and spouses. The conclusion is that although there are custodial services, they are severely limited both by availability and financial resources.

THE VA AND EXTENDED CARE SERVICES

The VA does offer veterans limited extended-care services in some locations. Most services (those expected to continue beyond 180 days) are available only to veterans who *either* have severe *service-connected* disabilities *or* pass strict means tests on their *and their spouses'* income and assets. Most services are also subject to copayment based on means, up to $97 per day. The copayment also depends on the service provided and on the veteran's VHA priority group. Services are often not available everywhere, have long waiting lists, or are otherwise difficult to access. In sum, they are usually not relevant to any client who was not severely disabled in the line of duty and whose goal is to avoid impoverishment if he needed care.

HOME-BASED PRIMARY CARE

The VA's highly regarded Home-Based Primary Care (HBPC) program is "a home care program that specifically targets individuals with complex chronic disabling disease, with the goal of maximizing the independence of the patient and reducing preventable emergency room visits and hospitalizations. HBPC programs provide comprehensive primary care by an interdisciplinary team in the homes of veterans with complex chronic disabling disease, who are not effectively managed by routine clinic-based care. HBPC is very different from and complementary to standard skilled home care services, in population, processes, and outcomes. HBPC targets persons with advanced chronic disease, rather than remediable conditions[1]."

This program is widely commended for improving outcomes while reducing costs and was suggested as an example for Medicaid to emulate. Last year, it dropped its copayment requirements[2] and is now available in three-quarters (116 of 152) of VA hospitals.[3]

Nonetheless, in practice, the program is poorly accessible to veterans who need extended care. It currently serves just 12,000 of the almost nine million people enrolled in the VA health care system.[4] Although it does not impose Medicare's requirement that the patient be *homebound*, it is dwarfed by the 3.5 million patients who receive Medicare-funded home health care even with this restriction. HBPC's other requirements follow:

- A complex, chronic disabling disease that necessitates care by an interdisciplinary team

- High risk for recurrent hospitalization or nursing home placement

- Determination by the HBPC team that the home is the most appropriate venue for care

In practical terms, the above means that HBPC's participants are among the sickest in the VA health system, with an average of 19 clinical diagnoses and

15 medications. A patient who simply needs assistance with ADLs or is cognitively impaired stands little chance of being admitted.

NURSING HOME SERVICES

The VA offers three types of extended-care benefits:

1. VA Community Living Centers (formerly termed "VA nursing homes")

- Stays beyond 90 days typically are available only to veterans rated 70% disabled or 60% disabled and unemployable.

- Patients whose disabilities are not service-connected must pass admission means tests on assets and income.[5]

- Patients without severe disabilities are accommodated as space and resources permit, with priority given to veterans with service-connected disabilities and those who need post-acute-care rehabilitation.[6]

- Copayment based on means.

2. State Veterans Homes, which are operated by each state and receive partial VA funding

- Admission criteria vary by state; the VA will not pay for veterans' non-veteran spouses and parents even if the state does.

- Means-tested admission; standards vary by state.

- Copayment based on means; standards vary by state.

- Long waits of weeks or months for admission are typical, sometimes more for Alzheimer's units.

3. Adult Day Health Care

Adult Day Health Care (ADHC) is similar to other adult day care programs, providing skilled services, case management, and assistance with ADLs or instrumental activities of daily living (for example, preparing meals and taking medicines). It is for veterans who need such services, who are isolated, or whose caregiver is experiencing burden. ADHC may be provided at VA medical centers, state Veterans Homes, or community organizations.[7] As part of the VHA Standard Medical Benefits Package, ADHC does not means test to determine admission but:

- Does require copay based on means
- Is not available everywhere
- Admission is based on clinical need

DOMICILIARY CARE PROGRAM

VA provides custodial care at home under the Domiciliary Care Program. The primary funding mechanism is the Aid and Attendance Pension (also known as the Enhanced Pension, Improved Pension, or Special Pension), available to those veterans who do not have service-related disabilities and have limited means.

AID AND ATTENDANCE PENSION

The Aid and Attendance Pension (referred to as the A&A program) is for veterans who meet strict service, income, and asset criteria (see below).[8] The program offers modest compensation for veterans over 65 and surviving spouses who require the regular attendance of another person to assist in performing activities of daily living or have a substantial cognitive impairment. The applicant's physician must confirm that his or her physical or cognitive condition has deteriorated to the point that the applicant requires daily assistance from others.

A&A is a pension benefit, offered independently of any service-related injuries. If all requirements are met, the VA determines eligibility by examining the veteran's or surviving spouse's total household income, excluding unreimbursed medical expenses. If the remaining income amount falls below the annual income threshold for the benefit, VA pays the difference between the claimant's household income and the Aid and Attendance threshold.

SERVICE CRITERIA

The veteran must have been on active duty for at least one day during the official periods of World War II (July 12, 1941–December 31, 1946), the Korean War (June 27, 1949–January 31, 1955), or the Vietnam War (August 5, 1964–May 7, 1975), and served at least 90 days of total active duty.

The eligible arms of service are the Army, Navy, Air Force, Marines, Coast Guard, and (for World War II) ocean-going Merchant Marine civil-service crew. The veteran must have been discharged under honorable conditions to be eligible.

FINANCIAL CRITERIA

INCOME

The household income of the veteran or the surviving spouse cannot exceed the Maximum Allowable Pension Rate (MAPR) for that category of application. Go to http://nationalincomelimits.vaftl.us/ to determine your income limit based on where you live.

The household income can be reduced to meet the income test under certain special conditions. Households earning $2,000 to $6,000 a month or more might still qualify even though their income does not meet the income test.

ASSETS

As a general rule, household assets cannot exceed $80,000. But there is no specific test in the regulations. Veterans service representatives in the regional office are required to file paperwork justifying their decision if they allow assets greater than $80,000. Thus, this amount has become a traditional ceiling.

Concerning the asset test, the service representative is encouraged to analyze the veteran's household needs for maintenance and weigh those needs against assets that can be readily converted to cash, and whether the income from that cash will cover the difference in the household income and the cost of medical care over the care recipient's remaining life span.

In the end, the decision concerning allowable assets is a subjective one made by a service representative. In certain cases, a benefit award could be denied unless assets are below $20,000 or even $10,000.

A personal residence, a reasonable amount of land on which it sits, personal property, and automobiles for personal use are exempted from the asset test.

Recent proposed changes will have a substantial impact on eligibility. Unlike Medicaid eligibility requirements (see Chapter 6), the VA had not employed a "look back" period and resulting penalties from receiving benefits if transfers were made within a specified period. That is about to change in 2016 if proposed regulations are adopted.

Generally, the VA will track net worth asset amounts (see details in Medicaid section). It will also, as with Medicaid, look at annual income in determining eligibility. But unlike Medicaid, income and assets will be combined.[10] It is strongly recommended that you contact the VA and secure the advice of an attorney who specializes in the field.

BENEFIT

A&A benefits are paid tax-free. They increase with inflation, but have increased by only 1 or 2% in total since 2008. The benefit in 2016 is:

$1,788 for an unmarried veteran

$2,120 for a married veteran or a veteran with one dependent

$1,149 per month for a surviving spouse

HOMEMAKER AND HOME HEALTH AIDE CARE

The VA provides Homemaker and Home Health Aide services under contract, but again with strict limitations:[11]

- The patient must need assistance with at least three ADLs, or have significant cognitive impairment, or have a more complex combination of conditions.

- Patients with at least 50% or service-connected disability receive priority.

- Continued need for services evaluated every six months for first year and annually thereafter.

- Means testing at acceptance.

- Copayment is based on means.

- The program is not available everywhere.

HOSPICE AND PALLIATIVE CARE

Hospice is a comfort-based form of care for veterans who have a terminal condition with six months or less to live. *Palliative care* is a form of treatment that emphasizes comfort care but does not require the veteran to have a terminal condition. These services are available to those who meet the clinical need, without means testing or copayment.

POWER THOUGHTS

• The VA provides primarily skilled and rehabilitative care. The programs that do pay for custodial care are limited and usually means tested. The VA takes into consideration your assets and income in determining if it will pay for care.

REFERENCES

1.) Julie Leftwich Beales and Thomas Edes, "Veteran's Affairs Home Based Primary Care," *Clinics in Geriatric Medicine* 25, no. 1 (2009): 149.

2.) Emily White, "Veterans Affairs Eliminates Copayment to Increase Patient Access to Skilled Home Healthcare," *Partnership for Quality Home Healthcare*, May 7, 2012, http://www.homehealth4america.org/media-center/52

3.) Emily Egan, "VA Home Based Primary Care Program: A Primer and Lessons for Medicare," *American Action Forum*, November 1, 2012, http://www.americanactionforum.org/wp-content/uploads/sites/default/files/VA%20HBPC%20Primer%20FINAL.pdf.

4.) Ibid.

5.) "Nursing Homes for Veterans," *National Care Planning Council*, February 26, 2009, http://www.longtermcarelink.net/article-2009-2-26.htm#.

6.) Ibid.

7.) "Geriatrics and Extended Care: Adult Day Health Care," *US Department of Veterans Affairs*, January 8, 2016, http://www.va.gov/GERIATRICS/Guide/LongTermCare/Adult_Day_Health_Care.asp#.

8.) *VeteranAid.org*, 2016, http://www.veteranaid.org/.

9.) John L. Roberts (Certified Elder Law Attorney) in discussion with the author.

10.) Ibid.

11.) "Homemaker/Home Health Aide," *PN Online*, March 31, 2016, http://pvamag.com/pn/article/3813/homemaker_home_health_aide.

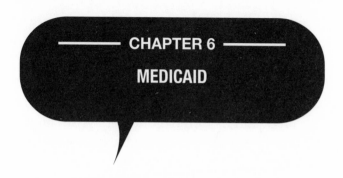

WILL MEDICAID FUND MY PLAN TO PROTECT MY FAMILY?

The short answer is that it may, but it has severe limitations and it is not free for those with certain types of assets and income.

A reminder of the two goals of the plan:

1. To allow you to remain safe at home while preserving the emotional and physical wellbeing of those you love.

2. To allow you to fulfill financial commitments.

As we analyze Medicaid, you will quickly notice its limitations.

MEDICAID OVERVIEW

Because of the similarity of their names and common history, Medicaid is often confused with Medicare. Their roles in funding extended care, however, are quite different.

Table 3. Medicare v. Medicaid	
Medicare	**Medicaid**
Pays for skilled and rehabilitative care	Pays for skilled and rehabilitative care
Is funded by taxes on participants	Is funded by the state and federal governments
Does not cover custodial care	Covers custodial care but primarily in SNFs
Is an entitlement program	Is means tested

THE HCBS AND PACE WAIVER PROGRAMS

Medicaid does pay for care in the community—services at home, adult day care, and assisted living—under a federal waiver program for which states may apply,[1] known as Home & Community-Based Services (HCBS).[2] For those 55 or older, there is the similar Program of

All-Inclusive Care for the Elderly (PACE). At first glance then, it appears that Medicaid would be a formidable competitor. A closer look proves just the opposite.

The criteria for Medicaid eligibility include:

- **Assets** must generally be under $2,000 and **monthly income** generally under $2,163 per month.

Few states have a look-back period for care in the community. You can likely qualify under the first criterion by giving assets away. The question is, what kind of assets are being gifted?

- If qualified funds, then there is an immediate federal and state tax.

- If low-cost-based assets, then there is an unnecessary capital gains tax. Had the money been in the individual's name at death, there would have been a free step-up to fair market value; the value of the investment at date of death would become the new cost basis.

If you are still inclined to gift assets, the next hurdle is income. If you have more than $2,163, then you generally do not qualify.[3]

No attorney who understands Medicaid will tell you that these various home care programs are a viable source to pay for care in the community.

Therefore, if your goal is to remain in the community, Medicaid is not a viable resource to pay for care.

MEDICAID ELIGIBILITY[4]

There are only two criteria: assets and income.

ASSETS

Assets are divided into three categories:

    1. Countable assets (called *non-exempt* or *available assets* in some states)

    2. Non-countable (also called *exempt*) assets

    3. Inaccessible assets

COUNTABLE ASSETS

Countable assets are any personal financial resources owned or controlled by the applicant for Medicaid benefits. Medicaid considers them available to pay for care.

They include:[5]

- All investments (stocks, bonds, real estate, etc.)

- Annuities unless they have been annuitized, then the annuity is considered income

- Cash value in life insurance if the death benefit exceeds $1,500

- All cash, certificates of deposit (CDs), money market, checking, and other liquid funds

- All tax-qualified pension plans if applicant is retired and it is not in payout status

- All other residences

NON-COUNTABLE ASSETS

Non-countable assets are acknowledged by Medicaid but are not used in determining eligibility.

They generally include:

- A primary residence, if the net value exceeds a cap, set by the state, of either $552,000 or $828,000 in 2016 and a spouse does not live in it

- A prepaid burial account

- Term life insurance

- A small sum of cash (the *cash allowance*), usually about $2,000

- Business assets if the applicant derives livelihood from them

- A car for personal use (some states cap its value)

- Personal items

INACCESSIBLE ASSETS

Inaccessible assets are assets that would have been countable but to which the applicant cannot gain access. They include, for example, stock in closely held companies and accounts that require the applicant to give consent to disbursement, but the applicant cannot because of dementia. In the latter case, the state gives the family a limited period of time to file a petition to obtain access.

THE LOOK-BACK AND INELIGIBILITY PERIODS

The look-back period is a time span used by Medicaid to review all transfers when an application for long-term care benefits is submitted. All states use a five-year period. Any gifts create a period of ineligibility that begins on the date an application is submitted, not the dates the transfers were made. States use the following steps:

1. All gifts made during a five-year period are aggregated. Let's assume that total is $100,000.

2. The total amount is divided by what your state considers the average monthly cost of a semiprivate room. Let's assume your state sets that figure at $5,000.

3. The total period of ineligibility would be 20 months ($100,000 / $5,000).

One option, then, is to simply give away assets and wait five years.

The financial issues are the same as with transferring assets to qualify for home care benefits.

• Immediate taxes on the transfer of qualified funds.

• Taxes on appreciated assets when sold. Assets with a capital gain (the positive difference, if any, between the acquisition and disposal prices) are not taxed if they appear in the individual's estate at death. However, if given away, they do incur a capital-gains tax liability, albeit a delayed one, when their recipients sell them.

MEDICAID TREATMENT OF COUPLE'S ASSETS

All countable assets in a marriage are considered jointly held and available to be spent on the institutionalized spouse's care, subject to certain spousal allowance limits. A provision called the *spousal impoverishment rule* allows the *community spouse* (the spouse who is not chronically ill) to retain a certain amount of assets and income.[6] Beyond this allowance, all of the couple's assets, earned by and held in the name of either spouse or jointly, are generally considered countable and available to fund the institutionalized spouse's care.

The community spouse's assets are considered countable even if:

- There is a premarital agreement.

- The institutionalized spouse never contributed to them.

- The couple lives in a community-property state (assets brought into the marriage are not subject to division in a divorce).

There is an exception to this rule in some states. If the community spouse has a tax-qualified plan that currently prohibits access, it may not be considered as part of the institutionalized spouse's assets. Please check your state policy on qualified plans for community spouses who have not retired.

COMMUNITY SPOUSE RESOURCE ALLOWANCE

A *snapshot* is taken of the couple's assets on the day a spouse goes into a medical institution or nursing home, where that spouse is expected to stay more than 30 days. The community spouse gets to retain a certain amount of those assets, calculated by the community spouse resource allowance (CSRA) formula.[7]

The CSRA was established to allow the community spouse to survive financially if his or her spouse needed SNF care. In 2016, the community spouse is allowed to keep half of the couple's combined assets, but:

- No less than a minimum (the *floor*) of $23,884.

- And no more than a maximum (the *ceiling*) of $119,220.

These amounts are adjusted yearly. States have the option of raising the floor; Florida, California, and Massachusetts are examples of states that have raised it from $23,884 to $119,220. In those states, the community spouse gets to keep the first $119,220 in combined assets.

EXAMPLE:

Alan and Rebecca, both widowed, marry. Prior to their wedding, they signed a prenuptial agreement to define what would happen to their separate holdings in the event of a divorce or death. Rebecca entered into the marriage with over $500,000. Alan brought his home and $220,000 into the marriage.

Alan suffers a serious stroke that leaves him paralyzed. After four years of trying to care for him at home, Rebecca places her husband in a nursing home on January 1, 2015.

The snapshot of their assets on that date shows $720,000 (remember, all assets are generally considered jointly held). To qualify for Medicaid coverage, the couple will be required to spend down their combined assets to *the maximum ceiling of $119,220. Medicaid will not recognize the prenuptial agreement.*

INCOME: INDIVIDUALS APPLYING FOR MEDICAID

All income, regardless of how earned or when received, is considered available to be spent on the Medicaid beneficiary's care, with three exceptions:

- A personal monthly needs allowance, usually between $30 and $60 per month, to cover such items as clothing, toiletries, and medical expenses not covered by Medicare or Medicaid

- Your Medicare Part B and Medicare supplement insurance premiums

- Other small deductions permitted by state law

SPEND-DOWN PROGRAM

More than half of the states employ a so-called spend-down program in which the beneficiary's monthly income goes to the nursing home. The only condition is that it must be less than the private cost of a room.

INCOME CAP STATES

Remaining states cap the amount of monthly income a Medicaid applicant can have. They include:[8]

Alabama	Georgia	New Jersey	South Dakota
Alaska	Idaho	New Mexico	Tennessee
Arizona	Iowa	Oklahoma	Texas
Arkansas	Kentucky	Oregon	Wyoming
Colorado	Louisiana	South Carolina	
Delaware	Mississippi		
Florida	Nevada		

These states grant eligibility only if the monthly income of the applicant is at or less than a cap, generally $2,199 in 2016. Those whose income exceeds the cap do not qualify for Medicaid unless they establish a *qualified income trust*, commonly called a *Miller trust*.[9]

Here's how it works:

The trust, which is established either by the family of the applicant or the nursing facility, must have the following provisions:

- The beneficiary is the Medicaid applicant.

- The beneficiary's income is deposited into the trust.

- The trustee then distributes to the nursing home no more than $2,199 per month. The applicant is now at the cap and can qualify for Medicaid.

- The balance remains in trust and is paid to the state upon the beneficiary's death.

INCOME: COUPLES

The community spouse's monthly income is never used in determining the Medicaid eligibility of his or her institutionalized spouse.

MINIMUM MONTHLY MAINTENANCE NEEDS ALLOWANCE

Since most couples applying for assistance have minimal income, the state and federal governments (which jointly fund Medicaid) have attempted to leave those in the community with a livable allowance. The community spouse is allowed to keep a minimum monthly maintenance needs allowance (MMMNA).

The MMMNA in each state has to equal at least a floor of $1,991.25 in 2016 and can be as high as the ceiling of $2,980.50, depending on your state. These rules only apply if the community spouse's monthly income is less than the floor. If, for example, her income is $3,000 per month, she gets to keep all of it, but would not qualify for the MMMNA allowance.

Here's an example of how serious using Medicaid to pay for skilled nursing home care can be for people with assets and income:

Susan and Francis are in a second marriage. They have the following assets and income:

- *Susan has a $150,000 individual retirement*

account (IRA); Francis has an IRA converted from a 403b plan worth $100,000.

• Susan has stocks worth $100,000; Francis has stocks and bonds worth $171,220.

Total assets: $521,220.

• Susan receives $25,000 from her IRA and Social Security retirement benefit.

• Francis has a pension of $52,000 and investment income (including a drawdown of the IRA) of $15,000 per year.

Total income: $92,000.

They have a standard premarital agreement stating that in a divorce or at death, their assets would go to their children, not to each other.

Francis is diagnosed with early-onset dementia in 2011. After keeping him home for four years, Susan decides she has no choice but to place him in a nursing home in 2015. Here is what happens to their assets and income in Massachusetts:

There are two stages:

ASSETS

Medicaid takes a snapshot of the couple's assets when Francis is admitted to a nursing home. Susan gets to keep up to one-half but no more than a federal and state ceiling of $119,220. Most states allow her husband to keep $2,000 (varies by state), but it simply allows his wife to keep it for a total of $121,220.

Medicaid disregards premarital agreements. Therefore, the total Susan keeps is $119,220. The excess of $400,000, which includes her assets, must be spent on her husband's care.

Once the couple is down to $121,220, Francis will qualify for benefits.

INCOME

By law, Susan keeps her $25,000 but nothing from her husband's income. Therefore, his pension of $52,000 must be paid to the nursing home. The income from the IRA is extinguished because the asset had to be used to pay for his care.

Here is the result of their reliance on Medicaid:

• *The couple started with $521,220 in total assets. Susan is left with $121,220.*

• *The couple started with $92,000 per year in income. Susan is left with $25,000.*

TRANSFERRING ASSETS TO A TRUST

The second option is the use of trusts. A trust is a legal instrument established by an individual or couple to hold assets. The person funding the trust generally is referred to as a *donor* (or *grantor* if he or she transfers real estate). Assets held in the trust are for the benefit of persons called *beneficiaries*, and one or more *trustees* manage the trust.

All trusts must have at least:

• A donor or grantor who makes the initial rules of the trust and funds it with assets

• One trustee (the person responsible for making decisions about the trust)

• One beneficiary who will receive the benefit of the trust's assets

There are two basic types of trusts: *revocable* and *irrevocable*.

REVOCABLE TRUSTS

These instruments allow the donor to maintain control of the assets. He or she may modify or terminate the trust and is always able to receive the benefits of the assets held in it. Revocable trusts are primarily used to avoid probate and manage assets if the donor becomes incapacitated.

They are of no value in protecting assets. Both the federal and state governments take the position that if the applicant is the donor, assets in the trust are countable and must be spent on care.

IRREVOCABLE TRUSTS

An irrevocable trust bears many of the same characteristics as a revocable trust. The one notable difference involves the donor's control over it. As the title suggests, an irrevocable trust, once established, may not be revoked or changed in any manner by the donor. The donor has no control of, or interest in, the assets.

Because of this characteristic, irrevocable trusts were widely used in Medicaid planning. To understand the issues involved in transfers to irrevocable trusts, it is helpful to review the history of their use.

IRREVOCABLE DISCRETIONARY TRUSTS BEFORE 1986

The most popular type of trust was commonly called an *irrevocable discretionary trust*. It typically worked like this:

- The donors created an irrevocable instrument and placed assets in it.

- They named themselves beneficiaries.

- They named a family member as the trustee.

- They gave the trustee authority to distribute all or none of the principal and interest at the trustee's discretion.

The underlying assumption was that if one of the donor-beneficiaries needed skilled nursing care and wanted to apply for Medicaid, the trustee would exercise his discretion and not make the principal and interest available to him.

ISSUES CREATED BY THE USE OF TRUSTS

- A trust cannot hold qualified funds. Funding it with these assets creates an immediate tax liability.

- The trust is of no value while the person needing care is in the community, because Medicaid pays only for limited, if any, custodial care.

- Once an applicant is on Medicaid, as previously explained, his or her community spouse loses most, if not all, of the applicant's income.

COBRA '85: CONGRESS STEPS IN

Congress restricted the use of irrevocable discretionary trusts in the Consolidated Omnibus Budget Reconciliation Act of 1985 (COBRA '85), effective in June 1986.[10] A trust will be classified as a

Medicaid qualifying trust, which means its assets are not protected, if:

- The trust is established by the applicant or the applicant's spouse other than by will and provides that either or both are beneficiaries.

- The trustee has been given discretion to distribute income or assets to either or both beneficiaries; Medicaid will presume that the trustee will do so.

- Medicaid deems those assets countable, which means they must be spent on care.

This legislation is *retroactive*.

TRUSTS ESTABLISHED BETWEEN *1985* AND *1993: INCOME-ONLY TRUSTS*

Attorneys shifted their planning strategies away from income-and-principal discretionary trusts and came up with an *income-only* instrument.

The concept is simple enough. Set up the same type of trust that was prohibited in 1985, but leave out one feature: discretion over principal. Such income-only trusts immediately became popular among Medicaid planners, because the state could not force the trustee to distribute principal. They typically worked like this:

- The donors created an irrevocable trust and placed assets in it.

- They named themselves beneficiaries.

- They named a family member as trustee.

- They gave the trustee authority to distribute all or none of the income at the trustee's discretion.

If one of the donor-beneficiaries needed skilled nursing care and wanted to apply for Medicaid, only the income was available to be spent on him, and only half of it was available if there were two beneficiaries.

TRUSTS AFTER OBRA '93

The 1993 Omnibus Budget Reconciliation Act (OBRA '93) again attempted to correct the perceived weaknesses of the 1985 law. The act has several provisions, the most important of which are:

EXPANDING ESTATE RECOVERY

The most far-reaching section of OBRA '93 is the law implementing *estate recovery*. This undermines those who have:

- **Income-only trusts drafted after August 11, 1993.** The entire proceeds of such a trust could be deemed available to repay Medicaid. As a practical matter, few if any states have implemented the law.

- **Life estates.** These are created when the owner of real estate conveys it to another person (usually a child or children) but keeps the right to live there and control what happens to it during his life.

Legally, the individual has conveyed a *remainder interest*, keeping a *life interest (also called a life estate),* which terminates at his death. The entire value of the property is included in the decedent's taxable estate at death, thereby giving the children a step-up of the property's cost basis to fair market value.[11] There appears to be no legal basis for estate recovery, but a few states have attempted to do so.

It should be noted that the above interpretation of the laws vary by state. For example, some states allow the use of a so-called a Medicaid Asset Protection Trust, which works because it severely restricts access to income and assets. As mentioned, you are well served to work with an elder law attorney.

MEDICAID PLANNING MAY BE ABLE TO PROTECT ASSETS, BUT RARELY INCOME[12]

Things to consider when you go to a Medicaid planning seminar, where the attorney tells you Medicaid will pay for your care:

• Attorneys tend to focus on protecting assets, not income, which is essential to support.

• Attorneys tend to focus on shifting assets. Would they do so if those assets were tied up in qualified tax-deferred investments and low-cost-based assets?

• Attorneys tend to focus on Medicaid paying for nursing home care, not care in the community, because the program has severe restrictions on income and assets.

POWER THOUGHTS

• Medicaid is a means-tested program. You have to have limited assets and income to qualify for benefits.

• Medicaid will pay for custodial care, but almost exclusively in a skilled nursing home, which is never the goal of an extended care plan.

• Medicaid will pay for custodial care at home, but benefits are limited and income has to be below about $2,100 per month.

• If you want to qualify for Medicaid, simply give your assets away and wait for the look-back period of five years to expire. The problem is that Medicaid is not free. Transferring low-cost-based assets and qualified funds creates immediate and future taxes.

• Medicaid planners can protect assets but they cannot protect income, which means most if not all of your pension, annuity, or Social Security would have to be spent on your care in a nursing home.

• Trusts are of limited use if you have qualified assets because transferring them into the instrument creates an immediate tax.

REFERENCES

1.) Eligibility and benefits vary by state.

2.) 42 U.S.C. § 215 (c).

3.) Some states (New York being the most prominent) allow the applicant to set up a so-called Pooled Disability Income Trust to hold the excess. This is quite complicated, and it suggested that you secure competent legal counsel to assist you.

4.) This section is a general description of eligibility. There are substantial differences in how states look at assets.

5.) 42 U.S.C. § 1382b.

6.) 42 U.S.C. § 1396r-5 (e)(2).

7.) 42 U.S.C. § 1396a (a)(10)(A)(ii)(V).

8.) New Jersey waives the cap if the applicant is already institutionalized.

9.) 42 U.S.C. § 1396p (d)(4)(B).

10.) 42 U.S.C. § 1396 (a)(k)(10).

11.) 26 U.S.C. § 2031.

12.) New York allows for the creation of a Pooled Disability Income Trust.

CHAPTER 7

WHAT IS LONG-TERM CARE INSURANCE?

Although I am not licensed to sell insurance products, I frequently work with insurance carriers who seek to educate financial advisors and insurance professionals about the subject of extended care and how a long-term care insurance product may be an appropriate solution.

Chapters 4-6 reviewed what you may have thought would pay for care. Chapter 7 takes a look at a product that is often misunderstood by the media and the public. If you have looked into or been solicited for long-term care insurance, you likely have received a substantial education about what lies in your future including, among other unpleasantries, decrepitude, dependency, and senility, all leading eventually to a nursing home that can quickly bankrupt you and your family. The point, of course, is to convince you to purchase an insurance product to cover the cost.

The presumption is that the more you are worried of the risk of the event, the more motivated you become to purchase a product to cover the cost of paying for it. It's rarely effective. The reality is that those who buy long-term care insurance are not motivated by the risk, but generally by three factors:

1. Prior experience: The emotional, physical, and/or financial consequences of previously providing care to a parent or other family member were so severe that the individual wants to make sure his or her family doesn't experience it in a following generation.

2. Immediate need: Individuals now want the product because they need it due to a serious health issue.

3. Commitment to another: Those who had no interest in proactively purchasing the product (typically men) but had the good sense to listen to their spouses or those they respect and/or love.

Almost no one who has benefited from long-term

care insurance will tell you they expected to use the product. So why do people purchase a product they never expect to use? They understand the serious if not irreversible emotional, physical, and financial consequences to those they love if they ever did need it but didn't have the plan in place. In other words, while they may believe that the *risk* of needing care is zero, the negative *consequences* to their family would be one hundred percent if they fail to take action by creating a plan.

Long-term care insurance is nothing more than a funding source for the plan. This makes perfect sense for a man. He won't buy the product to protect him from the risk of needing care, but will take steps to protect those he loves from the consequences of providing it to him if he does.

Long-term care insurance protects your family by providing a predictable stream of income in the form of a daily or monthly payment to fund the plan to keep you safe at home, while mitigating the two sets of consequences from providing care that will impact those you love.

EMOTIONAL AND PHYSICAL CONSEQUENCES

The income pays for your family to hire professionals to provide your care, allowing those you love to supervise it. This has the positive impact of keeping you home longer because there is far less stress. If there are children, they likely will not be under pressure to put their lives aside because they know you are safe and their mother or father is not buckling from the stress of providing care for his or her spouse. This brings us to perhaps the most important benefit of owning this product: *You have just given your children a second gift of life.*

The first gift was bringing them into this life. The second is letting them know that it is not their responsibility to put that life aside. It also helps keep the children together by keeping them apart. It is far better to have them continue with their lives than to force them together with no form of egress for years on end. The nightmare situation is for them to argue, bicker, and disagree over who will take care of you, where care will be given, and who will pay for it.

Having the proper plan in place and funding it with long-term care insurance mitigates the first set of consequences: the family remains intact and healthier than they would be if there were neither.

FINANCIAL CONSEQUENCES

If there is a stream of income to pay for care, there is no need to reallocate existing cash flow. This means you can sustain financial commitments. Since someone else is paying for care, there is no need to deplete your capital, which means (A) it can continue to generate income and (B) it is available to a surviving spouse, children, and, if you choose, charities or others.

So, in the final analysis, purchasing long-term care insurance has nothing to do with protecting you. It's recognition that protecting and providing for those you love is a lifetime commitment, one that should not end at an unexpected need for care. It is, simply put, an expression of love.

POLICY TYPES

There are many innovative products available to fund a plan. As such, we will refer to them as *extended care solutions*. Generally, long-term care policies come in five designs:

1. Individual or "traditional" long-term care insurance

2. Linked benefit

3. Annuity based

4. Life insurance with long-term care accelerated benefits

5. Life insurance with chronic illness benefits

INDIVIDUAL LONG-TERM CARE INSURANCE

As the name suggests, this policy covers only one person. It is referred to as traditional long-term care insurance because it has only one function, funding a plan to pay for care. Without exception, such policies offer a pool of funds that is determined by choosing a daily benefit (usually between $50 and $400 per day) and multiplying it by a number of years (usually between 3 and 10). You can "stretch" the benefit period by taking less than the daily maximum. For example, if you choose $200 per day for three years but only use $100 per day, the benefit period lasts six years. Other built-in features add flexibility, as these policies offer benefits that non-traditional policies generally do not. These benefits include:

• **Sharing provisions:** With a few exceptions, carriers offer a rider that allows one insured party to receive benefits from a related insured, if the first to use benefits exhausts his or her pool. If the individual dies without using benefits, generally the benefit period is added to the survivor's benefit period.

• **Care coordination:** Generally, some carriers designate a geriatric care manager, assigned at the beginning of a claim to help the family create a plan that includes where care will be given, who will provide it professionally, and how it will be coordinated over the years. Others allow the insured's family to make the choice.

• **Inflation adjustment:** This feature allows the daily benefit to keep pace with inflation. However, inflation adjustment makes the policy very expensive and generally should be avoided after age 57. The better alternative is to maximize the daily benefit and shorten the benefit period. For example, a $200 per day benefit for six years with 5% compound inflation for a 60-year-old male is approximately $8,000 per year. A $400 per day benefit for three years without inflation is approximately $3,500. For more information on this concept, work with an extended care planning specialist.

• **Home modification:** All policies provide funds to modify a house to allow the insured to remain at home longer.

• **Survivorship:** Many carriers offer the option of allowing a spouse's/partner's/sibling's policy to be paid up when the first insured dies.

To whom this policy may appeal:

• Those looking for flexibility and choices

• Those looking for affordability: Inexpensive for the value received if inflation is not chosen (Premium subject to change)

ASSET BASED

Also referred to as asset-based or hybrid products, the underlying asset is a universal life or whole life insurance policy. At the time of purchase, you choose the option of adding an additional benefits rider for extended care. You have to exhaust the death benefit first before accessing the rider. The long-term care benefit is paid either as a percentage of the death benefit or over a number of years.

Here is a general example of a premium of $105,000 paid in either a lump sum or from qualified (pre-tax) dollars.

• *Death benefit if not used: $150,000*

• *Long-term care benefit for 2 years: $150,000*

• *Continuation of benefits rider for 4 years:*

$300,000 (benefits only)

Ask your insurance professional if this type of policy can be written on a joint basis and/or offer lifetime benefits.

To whom this policy may appeal:

- Those who are concerned that the premium is wasted if the policy is not used because the beneficiaries receive the death benefit.

- Those who wish to receive a better rate of return on their premium, which is usually in a low-return investment such as a money market account or certificate of deposit to maintain liquidity. The death benefit will almost certainly be greater than what would have been earned from the bank or other institution. The insured also maintains liquidity (policy can be cancelled after a short period of time, usually three to five years).

ANNUITIES WITH LONG-TERM CARE RIDERS

These products are based on the use of a non-qualified annuity. The underlying asset is derived from either a pre-existing annuity or the purchase of a new one. You have the option of choosing a rider that automatically extends the value of the annuity for long-term care expenses for a period of either months or years. However, to access the benefits you must first exhaust the annuity and any growth.

How it works:

Example: *Using an Internal Revenue Code (IRC) procedure referred to as a 1035 exchange, you transfer, tax free, a non-qualified annuity worth $120,000 with a $60,000 cost basis (what you paid for the product with after-tax dollars) into a non-qualified annuity with a long-term care rider.*

> • *At time of purchase, you choose an extension of benefits from 1× annuity value to 2× value. Under IRC procedures, the payment for the rider, if taken from the annuity, is considered a 100% tax-free partial withdrawal from the annuity.*

> • *The contract continues to grow tax deferred.*

• If a claim is submitted, the insured uses the annuity first but pays no tax on drawdowns because of the provisions of the Pension Protection Act of 2006.[1] In effect, the government is giving you a substantial tax benefit because any partial withdrawals are considered fully taxed at the ordinary income rate.

• If the annuity is exhausted, the 1× option yields another $120,000 or the 2× option yields $240,000, paid over a preset period of months.

To whom this policy may appeal:

• May make sense for those with non-qualified annuities with substantial appreciation who want extended care benefits.

• An alternative for those who are willing to pay for care out of pocket. These products act as a "stop loss": After you have used the annuity, the carrier steps in, limiting your loss.

LIFE INSURANCE WITH AN ACCELERATED BENEFIT FOR EXTENDED CARE

These policies operate differently from the above asset-based or hybrid model, in that there is no extension of benefits past the death amount. Instead you simply draw down the purchased death benefit as care is needed.

How it works:

- A rider allowing the death benefit to be used for extended care is added to the insurance contract. Some carriers build the benefit into the policy.

- The death benefit is accelerated to provide tax-free benefits.

- What is not used is paid to the beneficiaries.

- Usually there is a minimum additional benefit if the death benefit is completely used for care.

To whom this policy may appeal:

• Those who have an additional need for life insurance. Be careful, however. You do not want to use this policy for extended care benefits if the death benefit is specifically earmarked for another purpose such as funding a special needs trust.

• Those who may not have substantial non-performing assets but very comfortable income and therefore can afford the premium.

• Those who want a traditional long-term care policy with modest benefits, keeping the premium low, but who are concerned that those benefits may run out.

For example, the insured purchases a $400 per day benefit for three years. At age 60, the premium is about $3,500 per year (vis-à-vis a premium of $8,000 per year for a $200 per day benefit for six years with 5% compound interest). The individual takes a portion of the premium saved for the shorter term of care and purchases a $100,000 death benefit with an accelerated rider for extended care. If the insured runs out of funds on the traditional policy, he or she has another $100,000 in benefits. If the policy is not used for care, the death benefit more than pays for the premiums.

LIFE INSURANCE WITH A CHRONIC ILLNESS RIDER

These life insurance–based products offer the opportunity of insuring those with preexisting health issues because of how they are underwritten. Typically, asset-based long-term care insurance underwrites for both the life insurance and extended care benefits. The former is based on mortality, which uses statistics to determine how long the individual is likely to live based on age and health. The latter is based on morbidity, which, simply stated, is how likely the individual is to become disabled based on current health and age and how long the illness will last.

With these contracts, the individual is generally underwritten only for the life insurance benefit at the time of issue. The underwriting for the extended care benefit, which is referred to as a *chronic illness rider*, is deferred until the insured makes a claim. The death benefit, like typical asset-based products, is used first, but how much you receive is based on your age and severity of diagnosis at the time a claim is made.

How they work:

You must present doctor certification that the condition you are filing a claim for will last for the remainder of your life. This is very different from other asset-based long-term care insurance products, in which you need only state that the condition is likely to last more than 90 days.

Policies pay benefits at the time a claim is filed in one of three ways:

1. Actuarial discount: In this model, the premium is waived at the date of claim and the death benefit, which is used to fund the chronic illness (CI) rider, is reduced based on the age of the insured. For example, a $100,000 face value contract is reduced to approximately $80,000 in CI benefits at age 70. The remaining $20,000 in death benefit is forfeited because it offsets the lost investment opportunity on the money being paid earlier than the anticipated death of the insured based on actuarial estimates.

2. Lien with interest method: In this model, the insured keeps paying the premium on the amount of the death benefit that is used to pay for care. In effect, the insured is paying interest that ends up being a lien against the balance of the death benefit not used for care. When the insured dies, the family may or may not receive a death benefit, depending on how much was used for care and the amount of interest.

3. Chronic illness premium: Unlike the other two options where no premium is added to the life insurance contract, this model charges one up front. The benefit is that the family receives the balance of any death benefit not used for care.

To whom this policy may appeal:

These policies are very effective if you have preexisting health issues.

TAX ADVANTAGES TO OWNING LONG-TERM CARE INSURANCE

The Internal Revenue Service (IRS) offers certain tax advantages to long-term care insurance. The rules are complex and it is strongly recommended that you consult with an insurance advisor to see if they apply to the purchase of your particular type of policy. Generally, here are the rules:

FOR INDIVIDUALS

The following rules are covered under IRC 213(d). You must file an itemized return. The premiums on long-term care insurance (LTCi) are considered medical expenses[2] and as such are subject to the 10% adjusted gross income rule (AGI). That is, to be deductible, the total of your non-reimbursed medical expenses (including the premium) must exceed 10% of AGI. Even then it is only the amount above this figure that can be deducted. For most individuals, this effectively eliminates any deduction. Even if you do qualify, the deduction is not absolute but is based on your age at the date of purchase. Currently, the figures, referred to as *Eligible Premiums* as of 2016, are:

40 and under	$390
40 to 50	$730
50 to 60	$1,460
60 to 70	$3,900
Over 70	$4,870

If you own a Health Savings Account (HSA) or Health Reimbursement Account, you can, without itemizing, deduct the Eligible Premium based on your age.[3] So for example, if the actual premium for a policy was $4,000 and you are 55 years old, you can write a check from your HSA for $1,460 and pay the balance from your personal funds.

If you are a participant in a so-called "Cafeteria" of "Flex Spending" account, the premium is considered an above-the-line deduction. That is, you have to pay the premium for the policy with after-tax dollars.[4]

FOR COMPANIES

There are four types of companies:

- **Self-employed**

- **Partnerships**

- **S-corporations**

- **C-corporations**

The first three are so-called pass-through entities; all profits and losses pass directly to the owners or shareholders. The same applies for benefits such as health insurance. The entities actually pay the premiums but ultimately those premiums are considered taxable income to the individuals who own or have majority shares.

Long-term care insurance premiums are treated like health insurance premiums. Here are the four steps:

1. The self-employed individual, partner in a partnership, or the shareholders in an S-corporation have their companies pay for the premium.

2. In turn, those entities issue either a K-1 for partnerships or a W-2 for S-corporations to the individuals who report it on their individual tax returns.

3. As with health insurance, all pay self-employment taxes.

4. Unlike health insurance, however, where the entire premium is then deducted from other income, the actual premium on a long-term care insurance policy is only reduced by the Eligible Premium based on age, leaving any balance to be taxed as ordinary income.

For example, the premium for a policy for Emily (age 54), a self-employed individual, is $5,000. Her company writes a check to the carrier for this amount, reducing gross income. However, at the end of the year, she must add that premium to her income. She then pays self-employment tax on that amount. But then, unlike health insurance where she could deduct the entire premium from her income, she is limited to only $1,460, leaving the balance to be taxed at ordinary income rates.

C-corporations are treated differently. The corporation can pay for the premium for an employee and deduct 100% of it from its gross income.[4] The premium is not attributed income to the employee, so no tax is due. If the individual goes on claim, like health insurance, there is no tax due on the proceeds.

A note about Limited Liability Companies (LLC): These types of entities are not tax filings but legal filings. They afford self-employed and partnerships liability protection that are built into S- and C-corporations. Therefore, if you are a LLC, you are likely filing as either a self-employed or partnership.

IMPACT ON PREMIUMS OF PENSION PROTECTION ACT

Starting in 2010, Section 844 of the Pension Protection Act provides for tax-free withdrawals from non-qualified annuities for payment of extended care. It also allows:

- 1035 exchanges (transfers are free of tax) of life-insurance cash value into life/long-term care hybrid contracts

• 1035 exchanges of life-insurance cash value into annuity/long-term care hybrid contracts

• 1035 exchanges of annuity value into annuity/long-term care hybrid contracts

• 1035 exchanges of life insurance or annuity value into single-pay long-term care contracts (which very few carriers offer)

STATE TAX BENEFITS[5]

States with no tax benefits:

• Georgia, Illinois, Kansas, Massachusetts, Michigan, Nevada, New Hampshire, Oklahoma, Pennsylvania, Puerto Rico (territory), Rhode Island, South Carolina, South Dakota, Tennessee, Texas, Utah, Vermont, Washington, and Wyoming.

States with tax benefits:

• Hawaii

The deduction is the same as federal tax law, subject to state adjusted gross income.

• Idaho

A deduction is allowed for premium paid.

• Indiana

A deduction up to the full cost of premium for the taxpayer and taxpayer's spouse paid in the taxable year.

• Iowa

A deduction is allowed to the limits provided in the federal Internal Revenue Code.

• Kentucky

Deduction from adjusted gross income allowed for any amount paid during the tax year for long-term care premiums.

- Louisiana

A credit totaling 10% of the premium is allowed against the individual's income tax.

- Maine

You are permitted a deduction as long as the amount subtracted is reduced by the amount claimed as a deduction for federal income tax purposes. Employers providing long-term care benefits to employees may also qualify for a tax credit.

- Maryland

Taxpayer is allowed a one-time credit of up to $500 against the state income tax. For employers, a credit up to an amount equal to 5% of the costs incurred by the employer during the taxable year.

- Minnesota

To be eligible for a credit, both of the following must be in place:

1. The policy must qualify as a federal deduction.

2. The policy has a lifetime benefit limit of $100,000 or more.

• Mississippi

A credit equal to 25% of premium costs paid during the taxable year for a policy for self, spouse, parent, parent-in-law, or dependent. The credit cannot exceed $500.

• Missouri

The taxpayer may deduct 100% of all non-reimbursed amounts paid for actual premium to the extent such amounts are not included in itemized deductions.

• Montana

Montana offers both a deduction for the entire amount of premiums covering taxpayer and dependents. The amount of the credit is based on the taxpayer's adjusted gross income and cannot exceed $5,000 per insured in a taxable year or $10,000 for two or more family members.

• Nebraska

The state permits a tax deduction for up to $2,000 per married filing jointly return or $1,000 for any other return to the extent that it is not deducted for federal income tax purposes.

• New Jersey

A deduction of premium may be taken if they exceed 2% of adjusted gross income and cannot be reimbursed.

• New Mexico

New Mexico permits taxpayers to claim a credit of up to $2,800 for medical care expenses, which includes long-term care insurance premiums if expenses equal $28,000 or more.

• New York

Allows a credit for 20% of premium paid for premiums. Employers are eligible for a credit equal to 20% of the premiums paid for employees.

• North Carolina

A credit is allowed for premiums paid equal to 15% of the premium costs, up to $350 for each policy based on published adjusted gross income limits.

• North Dakota

A credit is allowed for premiums of up to $250 per year.

• Ohio

A deduction of premiums for taxpayer, taxpayer's spouse, and dependents to the extent deduction is not allowed in determining federal adjusted gross income.

• Oregon

A credit is allowed equal to the lesser of 15% of premiums paid or $500. For employers, a credit of $500 is allowed for each employee covered by an employer-sponsored policy.

• Virginia

A policyholder may qualify for either a deduction or credit depending on federal filing status.

• West Virginia

A deduction for premiums to the extent the amount paid is not deducted in determining federal income tax.

• Wisconsin

A deduction is allowed for 100% of the premium to the extent it is not taken for federal income tax purposes.

REFERENCES

1.) Pension Protection Act of 2006 (Pub. L. 109–280).

2.) 26 U.S.C. § 7702 (b)(1).

3.) 26 U.S.C. § 220 (d)(2)(B).

26 U.S.C. § 223 (d)(2).

4.) 26 U.S.C. § 162 (a).

5.) Jesse Slome (Director of the American Association for Long-Term Care Insurance) in discussion with the author.

CHAPTER 8

THE CONVERSATION

The focus of this chapter is to give those of you who understand the subject and the consequences of providing care the ability to engage family members who do not believe the conversation is necessary.

The former would tend to be women and/or those with direct involvement with an individual who was so frail, so fragile from chronic illnesses, that he or she was no longer safe, resulting in serious emotional, physical, and financial consequences (see Chapter 1).

The latter tends to be healthy men who are generally "wired" to dismiss the risk of unexpected serious events happening to them. That being the case, they see no reason to plan for it. The goal is to give those of you who believe the conversation is essential the tools necessary to give those who do not compelling reasons to take action.

If you relate to the former, there are basically two approaches to engage the family member to the point of his (or her) making a decision to protect you and others. The first is referred to as a risk-based conversation. It can be reduced to three steps:

1. You take the time to research all the statistics available on the substantial risk of needing care and the cost.

2. You sit down your husband, father, uncle, or significant other and educate him about what you have learned. You focus on what is going to happen to him, and of course you, if care is needed and how it likely will have a serious financial impact.

3. You suggest, for example, that long-term care insurance will solve the problem.

If you have tried this with the men who have not been directly involved with providing care, you likely have been on the receiving end of classic objections, including:

- "It's not going to happen to me."

- "We can self-insure."

- "It's too expensive."

- "I'll simply shoot myself."

- "We have other priorities right now."

DIFFERENCES IN THE PERCEPTION OF RISK

It is important at this point to review how men and women perceive risk.

As discussed in Chapter 2, how you respond to the risk of an unexpected serious event in life, such as death, disability, or in this case needing extended care, is to a large degree determined by gender differentiation in human evolutionary history.

Men are generally hardwired to find food and protect those for whom they bring it home. Their brains are generally constructed to dismiss risk because it would undermine these basic directives. In their mind, there is no risk of needing care due to chronic illnesses. If there is no risk of needing care, why talk about a plan to deal with it? In fact, any discussion of these events makes them feel very uncomfortable.

Although women also believe they will not need care, they are predisposed to take a more nuanced approach. They are directly involved in the raising and nurturing of children and, as such, instinctively understand the emotional and physical consequences of doing so.

The result is that they view an unexpected need for care (or death, or disability for that matter) through an internal prism: They take the event and refract it into a kaleidoscope of consequences.

• They understand the emotional and physical impact on their spouses and children if they needed care.

• They understand the consequences to themselves and their children were their spouses to need care.

Let's put those beliefs into language that both men and women can understand: Men believe there are no *ifs*, *ands*, or *buts* of needing care. Since there is no risk, there can be no consequences to those they love. No consequences? Why spend time worrying about it? Women, when asked if they believe they will need care, will often hesitate and then answer... they *hope* they don't.

Why? Because men have the ability to separate risk from consequences whereas women see risk and consequences as inseparable: a risk is a consequence.

Do you begin to see how a risk-based conversation is problematic with men? If you are a woman, the likely presumption is that explaining the risk of needing care and what it costs will motivate him to buy a product to cover both. It doesn't, because he doesn't see the event happening (i.e., no risk). If there is no risk, what are the consequences? What happens next are the debilitating objections mentioned previously.

A DIFFERENT CONVERSATION: CHANGING THE FOCUS CHANGES THE RESULTS

Changing the focus of the conversation starts with

understanding what motivates decent men generally to create families. Numerous studies have shown conclusively that men want to take care of someone and by doing so they become relevant. In other words, they want to matter... to feel important to others. Creating a family is the perfect solution.

The absolute best way to motivate a person who loves his family is to shift the emphasis from what is likely to happen to *him* to a conversation about the serious if not irreversible consequences that providing care would have on *them*... his family. The idea is to educate a man about how an unexpected need for care would so seriously compromise him physically and/or cognitively that those he said he would take care of would have no choice but to put their lives aside to take care of him. The education process should include the following:

• The emotional and physical consequences caused by providing what amounts to 24-hour care 7 days per week.

• The likelihood that at least one of the children will have to put aside his or (more likely) her life, and the impact it would have on that child's family and relationship with siblings who do not help.

• The inability to keep financial commitments because paying for care would require a reallocation of income.

• The very real possibility that there will be a wholesale disruption of the retirement portfolio, causing lasting damage to a surviving spouse and/or children who may need an inheritance.

What follows are sample discussions that integrate these key points.

Wife Discussing the Subject With Her Husband

"Tom, I think we are at a point in life that we need to have a discussion about what would happen to me and the children if you needed care over an extended period of years."

"I really don't want to discuss it right now."

"I am not thrilled with the subject, but we have to."

"Why?"

"Because it involves not just my wellbeing but the kids'."

"What do you mean the kids?"

"OK, it starts with having an understanding of what extended care is. It's necessary because of illnesses that cannot be cured, like dementia and Parkinson's. As they progress, they so severely compromise you that the people you said you would take care of...us...will have no choice but to take care of you. And that's the problem. I'm worried that it would have such a negative impact on me that one of our kids would have to get involved. I can't imagine that you would want that."

"Of course not. They have their own lives."

"The problem is they won't have a choice. And it won't be all the children but likely Maria. We have to think about how disruptive it would be to her husband and children. We also have to think about what would happen to her relationship with her brothers."

"I really don't want to think about it, to tell you the truth, the whole thing is depressing. And by the way, this whole thing is based on my needing care, which I don't think I will."

"Tom, I am not suggesting that you will need care. This is not a discussion about the risk of it happening, but the consequences to us if it did."

"Are you trying to scare me?"

"Stop for a second. Let's take a look at this a different way. I believe you. I believe that you don't think you will ever need care, so let's get the risk of that happening out of the way. Zero risk. I am suggesting that we focus on the awful consequences to the children if I become ill taking care of you or I can't because I died or became seriously ill myself. What choice would they have? So I am suggesting that you look at this as a set of consequences, which would be one hundred percent to their lives and relationships with their siblings. I can see the possibility that they may never speak to each other again over this."

"I never thought about it that way. But look, we have enough assets to pay for care."

179

"I think we do also. But I've been thinking about what would pay for your care. It would come from income, but we are pretty much committed to expenses. If we used it, we may not be able to keep those commitments."

"We have enough assets though."

"We do, but let's play it out. The assets are used to generate income. I am really nervous that if we use them they won't generate income. If the illness lasts long enough there may be very little left."

"This whole thing makes me uncomfortable, but I never thought about it from the kids' point of view. What do you think we should do?"

"I think it starts with us both agreeing that we have to do something. We need a plan. I want to make sure that if either of us needs care, we can stay home. I want to make sure that taking care of me will not devastate you emotionally and physically, and the other way around. But more importantly, I want to make sure that our kids are not involved."

"I don't have an issue with anything you say. Are

you suggesting that we look into insurance?"

"That's part of it. We need to talk to someone who can explain the different types of products. Will you do that for me?

"Sure. Find someone we can talk to."

When you are discussing long-term care insurance in any form, do not focus on it paying for his care but rather funding a plan.

DAUGHTER DISCUSSING THE SUBJECT WITH DIVORCED FATHER

"Dad, I need to talk to you about something."

"About what?"

"About what happens to me if you ever needed long-term care."

"Appreciate the thought, but it's really not your concern."

"Dad, it is. Let's play it out. If you ever need care, mom

isn't going to do it. That leaves us. But it's not going to be 'us,' it's likely me. Please think about what it would do to my life, Paul's life, and to the kids. Think about what it will do to my relationship with Keith and Jon, who are not going to get involved. I can't imagine you want that to happen."

"No, but I told you I'll figure it out. It's not your concern."

"Please listen, Dad. It is my concern. What choice would I have?"

"Look, what if I don't need care?"

"I am not suggesting that you will. Dad, this is not a discussion about a series of risks that you face as you get older, because I get it... I get that you don't think these things will happen. Please look at this as a series of consequences to me, some of which could be irreversible. Do you think that I am going to have a great relationship with my brothers if my life comes to a stop while theirs continues?"

"You're serious, aren't you?"

"Dead serious. Look. The divorce was difficult enough for all of us. I just want a chance to spend my life focusing on my husband and kids. I love you. I want you to be safe. But none of this is going to happen if you need care and there isn't a plan to deal with it."

"Are you talking about insurance?"

"That's part of it. But just as important is thinking about a plan to allow you to stay at home and have professionals provide your care. That allows me to continue with my life, spending time only on supervising it. And, sure, insurance is important, but it's not to pay for your care."

"Why would you say that?"

"Because I know you absolutely believe you are not going to need care. The insurance isn't for you—it's for my brothers and me. It will keep us together by keeping us apart. Think about it. Do you want to place us in the position of arguing over who would take care of you and who was going to pay for it? Dad, think of why you bought life insurance. It wasn't because you thought you were going to die. It's because you loved us. That's how I would like you to think about long-term care insurance."

"What do you want to do?"

"I want your permission to speak to a professional about the subject and your promise that you will take it seriously."

"I never knew you loved me that much. Go ahead."

Never focus on the risk of needing care, only the consequences. Never focus on the product, only on the plan to mitigate the consequences. Never focus on anything happening to *him*, only *them* (you and the siblings).

SAME-GENDER COUPLES

Bill and his husband, Michael, are in their late 50s. Bill has two children, Peter and Michelle, from a first marriage. Michael has no children. Bill is estranged from Michelle, but has a close relationship with his son. Michael has provided hands-on care for his father, who recently died. Michael has a cordial relationship with both children and goes out of his way to avoid friction.

"Bill, I think it's time we talked about something we

both would rather not."

"What?"

"It's about making a plan to take care of each other if one of us ever needed care like my father did."

> *"I know what it did to you and your relationship with your sister. But we're only in our fifties, and frankly I am uncomfortable talking about it."*

"I am too, but if I have learned anything it is that this has nothing to do with me and nothing to do with you. It's something much bigger."

> *"What do you mean?"*

"I need to talk to you about what would happen to me emotionally, physically, and financially if you ever needed long-term care. A big part of that discussion has to include your children."

> *"Michael, I know we need to talk, but I told you not now. And about the kids, I am not looking for them to help."*

"We can't put it off. This has nothing to do with you needing care. I get it. I don't think I am going to need care either. And you know... my father didn't think he would. This is not a discussion about a series of risks you face as you age, it's a discussion about a series of consequences to me, our lifestyle, and your children."

"What do you mean?"

"Let's play this out: If you needed care... not when, but if... what do you think taking care of you would do to me?"

"I know it would be hard."

"It would. I can tell you that if you ever needed care, it would end up having a serious impact on my health as well. You know that happened to my mother trying to take care of my dad. It's not that I don't want to take care of you... I do. I love you with no 'buts' attached. I need your help in putting together a plan that protects me as well as you."

"I never thought about it like that, but I can't get my head around the issue of needing care."

"I am not asking you to. Look at it this way: You can still believe, as I do, that nothing is going to happen. So look at the risk as zero. No problem. Focus instead on the consequences to me and the children if you did need care."

    "How are the kids involved?"

"That's another set of consequences. Let's play that out as well: You need care. I take care of you. It starts to affect my health to the point that your son may have to step in."

    "I don't want him involved."

"Bill, what choice would he have? But the problem is that he has his own life, a family and a career. What choice would he have if he saw you were not safe? Then there are the repercussions with his sister. It's unlikely that she will help, which means Peter has all the responsibility. It's safe to say that if you ever need care your children may never talk to each other again. Then, there's the issue of paying for care. It's going to disrupt every plan we have worked on to make sure we are secure as we get older."

"Are you talking about long-term care insurance?"

"Not particularly. It's the plan, Bill. We need a plan to make sure the other is OK should either need care; that your kids do not have to put aside their lives and that they can continue to have a relationship with each other, and it's about keeping our financial commitments."

"What do you want to do?"

"I want to find a professional who can help us put together the right plan. Hopefully that person will also talk about powers of attorney and health care proxies so your kids know exactly what your wishes are, not what they think they are."

"OK."

SECOND MARRIAGES

Matthew, an attorney, and Dee, a nurse, are 61 and 55, respectively. This is a second marriage for both. Matthew has three children and Dee has one son. Their assets are held separately. Matthew has had a prior experience with providing care; Dee has not.

"Dee, I am starting to think about the whole subject of long-term care. The subject came up when I spoke to my sister about another matter, and I have to tell you she is still upset about my not helping with mom."

"I understand. Is there anything I can do?"

"The damage is done, but I am starting to play this out in my head and I don't like what I see if either of us needs care."

"You know I'll take care of you."

"That's the problem. I know you will. It's what taking care of me will do to your health emotionally and physically. It's not just you either. How do you think your son is going to react if he starts to see you have health issues taking care of someone who is not his father?"

"I never thought about it like that, but it's none of his business anyway; it's between you and me."

"Dee, he will make it his business. Now let's reverse it...

189

you need care. There is no doubt my kids are not going to like the fact that my health is declining because I am taking care of you."

"It could be a mess."

"Correct. And one more thing: Our assets are held separately. What do you think your son will say if any of your money is used to help pay for my care? The point is we need a plan."

"What is it?"

"It's to keep either of us safe at home while making sure that none of the kids are involved or have to worry about whose money is being used."

"Makes sense."

"I also want to explore long-term care insurance. My idea is that it won't just pay for our care, it will allow us to keep our assets separately. What do you think?"

"Let's look into it."

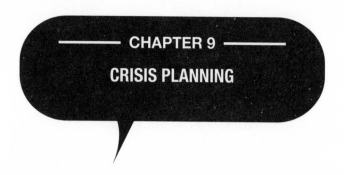

If you are at that point where a family member or someone close to you has been diagnosed with, or severely diminished by, a chronic illness, here are some ideas on how to protect at least a portion of the individual's estate.

TRANSFERRING BUSINESS ASSETS

If a Medicaid applicant owns a business and derives income from it, generally, all assets associated with the enterprise are exempt. This exemption can be critical in helping couples in which one spouse cannot qualify for long-term care insurance because of preexisting medical conditions. The business can be transferred to the healthy spouse, who continues to derive income from it. If the sick spouse needs Medicaid, the program will allow the community spouse to keep the business assets and, by definition, the income.

SPOUSAL REFUSAL

The federal government has mandated that states qualify applicants for benefits even if their community spouses fail (or refuse) to participate in the application process. It's referred to as the *spousal refusal rule*, because the community spouse refuses to pay for the care of the spouse applying for benefits.

Generally, an individual will qualify for Medicaid benefits under spousal refusal if any of the following conditions apply:

- The community spouse's whereabouts are unknown.

- The community spouse is incapable of providing the required information due to illness or mental incapacity.

- The community spouse lived apart from the institutionalized spouse immediately prior to institutionalization.

• The couple is in the process of a divorce.

The state, however, reserves the right to sue the community spouse for recovery of money that otherwise would have had to be spent on care. If the state does file suit, it is almost certain to prevail unless there are extenuating circumstances.

DIVORCE

Filing for divorce may achieve the goal of protecting more than the 2016 spousal limit of $119,220, but there are two factors to consider:

• Couples in long-term marriages are extremely reluctant to file for divorce.

• The court of competent jurisdiction is not likely to strip the institutionalized spouse of all the assets.

Generally, a divorce should work if there is a premarital agreement that has already divided the assets.

Remember, however, that a premarital agreement will not work when applying for Medicaid.

DISABLED CHILD

All states allow the assets of an applicant that would have to be spent down on care to be gifted immediately to a child who is blind, under 21 or disabled, as defined as being on Social Security disability income. There is no look-back period. If an adult child is not capable of handling assets because of an intellectual disability, a Supplemental Needs Trust (also referred to as a *Special Needs Trust*) can be created to hold the resources if the applicant is under 65.

This type of trust is a complex instrument that if established correctly allows the applicant to qualify for Medicaid immediately while allowing the child to continue receiving state Medicaid benefits. The Trust can be used to pay for any reasonable expense of the child. Again, it is strongly recommended that you consult with an attorney who specializes in special needs planning.

MEDICAID ANNUITY

This type of annuity protects excess assets in the name of an applicant individually or his or her spouse from being spent on nursing home care.

Structure of the annuity: The annuity...

- Must be issued by an insurance company.

- Has to be for a period certain; life or life with period-certain annuities are not allowed.

- Has to be actuarially sound for the person who is annuitizing it.

- Cannot be assigned and must be irrevocable.

INDIVIDUAL USE

The applicant can take the excess of his or her personal cash allowance (generally $2,000) and purchase this type of annuity. However, the state must be named beneficiary for any amount paid.

Example:

Mark, a widower, is 80 years old. He is no longer safe, so his daughter decides to make a placement in a skilled nursing home. The private pay rate is $400 per day. Mark has $350,000 in cash and $2,500 a month in Social Security. Without an annuity, he has to spend-down his assets.

His daughter visits an attorney and is told that she can purchase an immediate Medicaid annuity. Here is the structure:

1. The $350,000 is reduced to cash.

2. The insurance company uses Medicaid guidelines in creating a period-certain annuity. At his age, the period is eight years.

3. The daughter commits the funds to the company who issues the annuity naming the state as the primary beneficiary with herself as the secondary; she gets what is left after Medicaid is reimbursed.

FOR A COUPLE

Under Medicaid guidelines for couples (see Chapter 6) the spouse at home can keep no more than $119,220. The procedure is to take the excess of this amount and transfer it into the name of the spouse at home who then purchases the annuity.

Example:

Peter is applying for Medicaid to pay for his nursing home care. He and his wife, Ellen, have $721,220 in assets. Under Medicaid rules, she keeps no more than $119,220 and his cash allowance of $2,000, which all states allow her to keep. This leaves a spend-down of $600,000 that must be spent on his care. Peter, through a power of attorney, transfers whatever funds he has to his wife's name, who then annuitizes everything except $121,220. She is, by law, allowed to keep all the income generated, and Peter qualifies for benefits immediately.

DOWNSIDE TO MEDICAID ANNUITIES

- Substantial taxes:

  o Transferring assets such as qualified funds creates an immediate tax at ordinary income tax rates.

  o Assets have to be liquidated to purchase the annuity, creating a capital gains tax.

- Market timing:

  o The investments may be down given the market, creating an actual loss versus a paper loss.

- Second marriages:

  o If assets are being transferred to a spouse with children of his or her own, who gets the income?

PROTECTING A PRIMARY RESIDENCE

Medicaid has the right in every state to place a lien on a primary residence if there is no spouse living there. If there is none, then a lien is immediately placed. However, no lien will be filed if any of the following conditions exists:

• The applicant's child is under 21, blind, or is permanently and totally disabled.

• The applicant's sibling has equity interest in the home and was residing in the home for at least one year immediately before the date the applicant became institutionalized.

• The applicant's child was residing in the applicant's home for at least two years immediately before the date the applicant became institutionalized and (as determined by the state) furnished the applicant care that permitted the applicant to reside at home rather than in an institution.

FINDING THE RIGHT ATTORNEY

It is strongly suggested that you consult with an elder law attorney who can expand on these ideas. The best place to find a professional in this field is to consult with a local Alzheimer's, Parkinson's, or multiple sclerosis society office or a local outlet of the Arc of the United States, which deals with intellectually and developmentally disabled citizens. All have a list of attorneys who have proven their worth to its members. Other resources include:

• The National Academy of Elder Law Attorneys (*www.naela.org*), a non-profit organization that has instituted a professional designation (Certified Elder Law Attorney, or CELA).

• The Academy of Special Needs Planners

CHAPTER 10

AUXILIARY LEGAL DOCUMENTS

No plan for extended care is complete without three critical legal documents: A durable power of attorney, a health care proxy, and living will. Very few clients have these documents, which can create any number of issues that could easily have been avoided if these instruments were in place.

POWER OF ATTORNEY

This legal instrument authorizes another to stand in your place regarding a wide range of transactions. There are three types: transactional, durable, and springing. The first is valid for a specific event such as authorizing your attorney or someone else to handle a real estate closing. The second type takes effect immediately and remains in effect until revoked. The third becomes effective only when you become incapacitated.

Choosing who is to be your representative for a durable power of attorney is not something to be taken casually. If married, generally your spouse would be appointed. If you are widowed or divorced with children, most people choose one of their children, but consideration should be given as to the relationship between the siblings. If they are fragile, it is essential that you, not the person appointed, inform the other children. They may not like it, but they will need to tolerate the decision. If you don't inform them and are no longer able to handle your financial affairs, and the appointed child announces that he or she will now take control, it is possible that one or more of the siblings may challenge the appointment.

The issue of whom you choose becomes more acute in second marriages. You may decide to appoint your spouse, which is fair enough. But have you considered how your children may react? You may argue that it is none of their business. Rest assured that they would consider it their business. Again, if you decide to do so, make sure you, not their step-parent, are the one to discuss it with your children.

HEALTH CARE PROXY

A health care proxy is a document that lets you to appoint another person, usually referred to as an agent, to convey your wishes and make health care decisions for you if you cannot speak for yourself. Whether they are legally binding or not depends on your state. As with a power of attorney, be very careful whom you appoint, particularly in a second marriage.

LIVING WILL

A living will is a written instrument that sets forth your wishes regarding continued medical care if you are in a coma with no reasonable expectation of survival. The document sets out that certain acts are or are not to be taken, such as amputation, resuscitation though extraordinary medical procedures, or the use of life support or mechanical devices. They are usually part of a health care proxy, and state laws vary on their enforceability. They are very effective in letting your doctors and family know your wishes.

A NOTE ABOUT DO IT YOURSELF LEGAL DOCUMENTS

There is no shortage of legal templates on the web, which you can use. Many sites state that they are straightforward and as such do not require the services of an attorney. Not true. These documents are often complex. It is strongly suggested that you seek counsel's advice.

MOVING FORWARD: MAPPING OUT YOUR PLAN

If you are a family member trying to engage someone you love in a conversation about extended care, it is best to map out your strategy. Here are some helpful ideas:

TAKE A MINUTE TO FAMILIARIZE YOURSELF WITH THE SUBJECT

Keep in mind that the person who is the object of the discussion, particularly if it is a male, does not want to hear about the risk of care because he or she deeply believes care will not be needed. Make sure you can quickly summarize what causes a need for care and use it only as an introduction to the consequences of providing it.

MAKE SURE YOU SHARE YOUR STRATEGY WITH KEY PEOPLE

For example, if you are child who wants to engage a parent, make sure other siblings are involved. There are a number of reasons to do so:

- You can ensure the right approach. Other siblings may have wanted to engage in the traditional approach of using risk and statistics to compel the parent to buy a product.

- You can neutralize sibling tension. By involving others in the process, it shows that you are not just trying to influence a parent to put you in charge of money or health care issues.

The point is that you want to be inclusive of your siblings' input. Your brothers and sisters will reinforce your conversation if the parent looks to a child to undermine your points.

CHOOSE THE RIGHT TIME AND PLACE

Bringing the subject up during a family event may not be the best timing. The individual will be preoccupied with arrangements and talking to others. Instead, consider setting up this conversation separately at the individual's home for a number of reasons:

• Family pictures: You can start the conversation by pointing to pictures of yourself and others that bring the individual back to a good place.

• The person's home is a safe haven giving him or her a sense of control and wellbeing. It puts into perspective what the individual has to lose in the absence of a plan. It is also an opportunity to explain how difficult it would be for him or her to get around.

YOU ARE NOT A TEACHER SPEAKING TO A CHILD

Be very careful not to have come across as if you are talking to a child. Avoid statements such as:

- "It's time we had a talk."

- "I think you need to really pay attention to what's going to happen if you don't listen to me."

- "How would it make you feel if I had to change your diapers?"

- "You know you are not getting any younger."

Instead, use statements that speak to what the individual, particularly a parent, has done during his or her life and how they want to continue to be relevant and provide protection:

- "I want to start by talking about how safe I felt growing up and how you and _____ raised all of us to be independent and make good decisions." The purpose of this statement is to show your love and respect and to create an opening to explain how you may have to put that life aside if care is needed.

- "This is not a discussion about you needing care as you age because I know you think you'll never need it. It's a discussion about a series of consequences to my life and my relationship with my brothers and sisters if you did." The goal of this statement is to have the individual "step outside of his or her self" to observe what would happen to those he or she promised to protect if care was ever needed.

• "I am proud of what you have done with your life and that you always took care of us. I can't imagine you would ever want to put us in a position where we would have to put aside our lives to take care of you." Once again, the statement compels the individual to think about the harm to others if the subject is not taken seriously.

NEVER TALK ABOUT A PRODUCT

The mention of a product is an immediate deal killer. The focus must always be on a set of consequences to those he or she loves if a plan is not created. If he or she states that you are trying to sell a product, respond with, "This is not a discussion about a product to protect you from an event that I know you don't think is going to happen. It's a discussion about what's going to happen to me and _____ if you ever need care."

FINAL THOUGHTS

For those who did not want to read *The Conversation* but took the time to do so, you have my respect. It's a tough topic to think about and I understand where you are coming from. I see on a daily basis the serious and damaging impact that providing and paying for care has on families, and I can assure you this book was a good use of your time. Hopefully, you will now proactively engage your family in a discussion and work together to create and properly fund a plan that protects the most important people in your life.

For those who have tried to talk to someone you love and found it difficult to inspire action, particularly if it is your dad, husband, or partner, perhaps *The Conversation* has given you insight to why and suggested a better approach. Remember, reluctance to creating a plan for extended care has nothing to do with his not caring. In fact, it is just the opposite. He cannot see himself not being available to take care of you and fulfill his obligations. Therefore, he dismisses the possibility of anything happening that would prevent him from doing so since, in his mind, the chances are zero.

In the end you will ask yourself, like I did and countless others who came before me, did I stay the course? Did I take care of those under my responsibility? Creating a plan for an unexpected need for care later in life is a wonderful way to make certain the answer is "yes."

INDEX